KU-572-667

Project management
Tools and techniques for
today's ILS professional

Barbara Allan

·1587791.

LIBRARY

ACC. No.
01098051.

DEPT. STAFF
LIBRARY

CLASS No.
025-1 ALL

UNIVERSITY
COLLEGE CHESTER

facet publishing

© Barbara Allan 2004

Published by
Facet Publishing
7 Ridgmount Street
London WC1E 7AE

Facet Publishing (formerly Library Association Publishing) is wholly owned by CILIP: the Chartered Institute of Library and Information Professionals.

Barbara Allan has asserted her right under the Copyright, Designs and Patents Act 1988 to be identified as author of this work.

Except as otherwise permitted under the Copyright Designs and Patents Act 1988 this publication may only be reproduced, stored or transmitted in any form or by any means, with the prior permission of the publisher, or, in the case of reprographic reproduction, in accordance with the terms of a licence issued by The Copyright Licensing Agency. Enquiries concerning reproduction outside those terms should be sent to Facet Publishing, 7 Ridgmount Street, London WC1E 7AE.

First published 2004

British Library Cataloguing in Publication Data
A catalogue record for this book is available from the British Library.

ISBN 1-85604-504-8

Typeset in 10/13pt Revival 565 and Zurich by Facet Publishing.
Printed and made in Great Britain by MPG Books Ltd, Bodmin, Cornwall.

Contents

List of tables

List of figures

Acknowledgements

Thank you to the many people in the information and library profession who have shared ideas, answered queries and generally discussed their project management experiences with me. Thank you to all the information workers who have shared their expertise and experiences in conference papers, articles and reports. These have provided examples of good practice throughout the book. A great many thanks must go to all the participants who have taken part in my Project Management workshops at Aslib/IMI and whose questions, comments and general experiences have helped me to develop my ideas and understanding of the topic. I would also like to thank Jenny Headlam-Wells for her generous feedback and help with Chapter 6. Finally, thank you to Denis and Sarah for providing me with their constant support during this project.

Part 1
Introduction

1

Introduction

The purpose of this chapter is to introduce project management in the context of information and library services (ILS) and to introduce this book. This chapter considers the following topics:

- What is a project? Different types of projects.
- What is project management? Its benefits and challenges. Different approaches to project management. Project management in ILS.

It also supplies an overall introduction to the book and an overview of the individual chapters.

This book

The aim of the book is to provide a practical guide to library and information workers who are involved in project work either as a project manager or as a member of a project team. Project work is widespread in all types of library and information units, and typical projects range from developing a new information service, moving a library and digitization to introducing a new staff development programme. Projects may be relatively small and simple, for example involving one or two members of staff working on the same team, or large and complex ones involving people working in multi-professional teams. Complex projects sometimes involve working across different boundaries – professional, organizational, geographical, or working with new and developing IT systems. ILS workers often carry out these projects alongside their 'full-time job' and find that they need to develop new skills and ways of working in order to successfully manage their project as well as their main work role.

The purpose of this book is to provide a guide and resource to project management within all types of information and library services (ILS). It explores tried and tested methods and techniques for managing projects and this includes paper-based approaches and also the use of project management software. Each chapter is supported by examples from a range of ILS departments and units. These examples provide a 'feel' for the realities of project management in today's turbulent environments.

This book is based on information and knowledge obtained and developed from:

- the author's experiences as a project manager in academic and workplace library and information units
- her experiences in project work as an independent consultant and trainer
- feedback from colleagues attending her project management courses based at ASLIB/IMI in the UK
- visits (both real and virtual) to a wide range of library and information services
- professional networks and conferences, and also the literature.

The traditional project management literature has developed from work in industry and military projects and, as a result, offers an approach that is embedded in the scientific management field. Much of it tends to assume that the project leader operates in a traditional authoritarian manner and is chiefly concerned with a top–down approach to managing the project. These traditional approaches to project management tend to be concerned with splitting the project into its constituent parts and then managing and controlling the project process. While it is important to analyse a project, produce and then implement a project plan, this approach to project management tends to under-emphasize the importance of people and the management of the relationships side of projects.

The author believes that project management is best achieved through co-operative and/or collaborative team work where the project manager's role is to facilitate and steer the process. If team members are active participants in all stages of the project process then they are likely to feel ownership for the project, commit themselves to it and work in a creative and effective manner. In addition many project managers are not the line manager of people on their project team and this means that they need to motivate and influence others through their leadership and management styles rather than through formal performance management processes. As a result, the 'soft' or human side of project management is considered an essential factor for success.

In this book the author has taken general project management tools and techniques and considered their use within the information and library field. In addition, she has explored the people side of projects in some detail and this includes working in different types of project teams and also virtual teams. The author is very aware that the library and information profession is a very broad one and this book is written to encompass the needs of project workers involved in large relatively well-funded national projects as well as individuals operating in workplace or school libraries with a very small (or non-existent) budget. As a result many of the tools and techniques offered in the book will be described in such a way that they can be implemented both by someone working with Post-it™ notes and pens and also by someone who is using the latest project management software.

This book is not intended to be read as a prescriptive guide to project management. It presents current ideas and models of good practice, and underpins these with a series of tried and tested project management methodologies. The book contains a range of examples and case studies, and these are meant to demonstrate current practice in a wide range of library and information units. One of the challenges of writing the book was identifying and selecting these case studies and examples as there were so many interesting and informative examples to choose from. After the reader has worked through this book or dipped into it, the author hopes that they will use the tools and techniques that are most relevant to their own professional context.

Projects and project work

What is a project? A very simple definition of a project is that it is a specific activity that involves innovation and change within the library and information service and that it has a clear aim, set of outcomes and start and end date. Using this definition projects could include:

- moving a library
- developing a new information service
- creating a new intranet site
- digitizing a collection
- merging two libraries
- building and moving into a new learning resource centre
- restructuring an information service
- developing a new marketing campaign
- re-cataloguing a collection
- producing a common training programme for a number of ILS
- developing a web-based information skills course
- carrying out research in an innovative area.

In all of these examples it is likely that the library and information workers will be operating with limited resources, e.g. staff, budget, time.

Sometimes participants on project management courses ask if work that they are carrying out in the library or information unit is 'project work'. For example, one academic librarian asked if their department's work on streamlining and standardizing their procedure manuals would count as a project. After some discussion it transpired that this task had a clear aim and outcomes (although these had never been written down), they had started the project as a result of discussions in a team meeting (so there was a specific start date) but no end date had been set. As a result the 'project' had drifted and this librarian and his team were all feeling de-motivated. One of the outcomes of this discussion was the realization that by calling the work a project, writing a project brief with a clear aim, outcomes and start and end date and using simple project management techniques then it would be relatively easy to re-motivate staff and complete the task. An e-mail sent to me a few months later confirmed that this was what happened in practice. So the action of explicitly identifying that something was a project and re-framing it in this way meant that it was managed as a successful project.

Different types of project work

The previous list of typical projects suggest that there are many different types of project work and these can be classified using the following headings:

- strategic or operational projects
- simple or complex projects
- local or distributed projects
- 'hard' or 'soft' outcomes
- fixed or changing environment.

Individual projects may fall into a number of these different categories. For example, the introduction of a new staff development process may involve a relatively simple local project that is supporting a strategic change. In contrast a digitization project may involve information workers operating in a complex distributed network that responds to strategic change at national and individual organizational levels.

Strategic or operational projects

ILS projects can be classified according to their level: those that take place at a strategic level and those that take place at an operational level. Strategic change is very distinctive and changes the direction of the organization. It may result in a changed mission and vision and will certainly result in new goals. Strategic change involves a major change and will have far-reaching impact on the organization, the staff and other stakeholders. This type of change normally takes place over months and years. Examples of strategic-level projects include:

- the merger of two distinct ILS services
- the introduction of a new appraisal scheme
- the introduction of new working conditions and practices.

Project management involving strategic changes is likely to involve the use of 'management of change' tools and techniques as well as project management ones. This is because such projects often involve a change in identity and culture of the library and information unit. This topic is considered in Chapter 8.

In contrast, projects that involve operational changes are less likely to result in major alterations, e.g. they may be located within a specific team or department and involve a relatively small change. These types of projects are likely to take place within a much smaller time frame, and while there is a need to manage the communication process the project manager and workers will not be involved in a major 'management of change' process. Examples of projects at an operational level include:

- the relocation of an office
- the refurbishment of an information service

- organizing a conference
- developing a new information service
- digitizing a collection
- re-cataloguing a collection
- developing a common training programme across a number of libraries
- developing a web-based information skills course.
- the introduction of a new web-based service
- the introduction of a new IT system into a department.

This classification is not absolute and if you are involved in project management it is worthwhile identifying which level you need to be working at. This is important as projects that lead to change at a strategic level tend to require a change in culture and attitudes. This involves a more in-depth management of change process than projects that take place only at an operational level. Project managers who are not aware of this difference may find that they are having to deal with a backlash to their project as a result of the cultural changes associated with the new strategy not having been addressed through the project management processes.

Simple or complex projects

At the start of any project it is worthwhile thinking about the level of complexity of the project. Projects can range from very simple ones to extremely complex ones. The more complex the project then the more important it is to use project management tools and techniques – these are the types of projects they were designed to support. In contrast, using these tools and techniques on relatively simple projects is rather like taking a sledge hammer to crack a nut. The time spent on using the methods would be better spent working on the project. Table 1.1 demonstrates the differences between simple and complex projects.

Table 1.1 Comparison of simple and complex projects

Characteristics	Relatively simple projects	Complex projects
	e.g. moving office, creating a new website or organizing a conference	*e.g. national digitization project, merging three libraries, implementing a new virtual learning environment*
People	Involvement of a small group of people who are all working in same building and organization.	Involvement of people from different professional backgrounds, different teams and organizations.
		Involvement of people with a range of first languages, from different cultures and who are living in different time zones.
		Involvement of a large number of different activities involving a number of different people.
Data	Relatively low volumes of data.	Involves large volumes of data.

Continued on next page

Table 1.1 *Continued*

Characteristics	Relatively simple projects	Complex projects
Risks	Risks can be easily identified.	Hard to identify risks.
Innovation	Low levels of innovation: while the project may be novel to the project team there is existing good practice in this type of work.	High levels of innovation.
Technology	Working with relatively well established and tested technology.	Working in a technical environment that is changing at a rapid pace.
Working methods	Use of tried and tested methods (even if they are new to the project team).	Working procedures established by an external body who may change them throughout the project.
Management	Project manager has complete control over project.	External body or another person may have real power, e.g. over timescale, resources, people. Responsibility for the project may be shared, e.g. by managers working in different organizations.
Environment	Well known to project workers. Little change in the environment over lifetime of project.	Turbulent with constant change caused by business environment, government or other external factors.

Local or distributed projects

Another consideration is the geography of a project. Many projects are located within an information service that is in one building – all the staff work there and all the project activities will take place within that building. In contrast, an increasing number of projects are distributed, e.g. across a campus or town, across a region or country, or perhaps they are an international project involving partners in different countries working across different time zones. Clearly a project located within one building is likely to be simpler to manage than an international project; the latter type is explored in more detail in Chapter 8.

'Hard' or 'soft' outcomes

Many projects involve the delivery of 'hard' or easily quantified outcomes, for example the relocation of a library or information service or the implementation of a new ICT system. These types of projects are more easily managed by using project management tools, described in Chapters 2 and 3, which involve breaking the projects down into discrete tasks and then planning to ensure that the project achieves its goals. These types of projects involve using techniques such as GANTT or bar charts, PERT diagrams and critical path analysis, which help to identify and plot the progress and relationships of project activities. In contrast projects that involve 'soft' outcomes, for example a change in attitude of staff, are less likely to involve the use of a wide range of project management tools and more likely to involve a series of development processes such as staff development events, team meetings and one-to-one coaching.

Fixed or changing environment

The final variable that needs to be taken into account is the environment of the project. The simplest type of environment is a fixed one where there is little change to the project parameters from beginning to end and also where the context of the project, i.e. the information or library service environment, is fairly static (as much as that is possible nowadays). In contrast some projects are located within a rapidly changing environment, for example the project outcomes may be changed or amended (the moving goalpost syndrome) or the ILS environment is extremely turbulent. In this type of situation the project manager and team has quite a challenging task, and the planning of the project process needs to take into account the need to maintain flexibility and to be responsive to the changing situation.

What is project management?

Project management involves using a range of management skills and techniques to successfully carry out a project. The types of activities involved in project management include:

- thinking ahead
- carrying out research
- planning what happens where and when
- managing the people and resources
- monitoring the project
- changing the plan
- communicating with people
- evaluating the project.

As mentioned earlier, the tools and techniques used in the project planning and management process were often developed by people who worked on major construction or defence projects. These projects are often extremely complex and involve the co-ordination and integration of the work of hundreds if not thousands of people. The traditional project management tools and techniques are focused around a project life cycle which typically involves the following stages:

- project initiation
- planning the project process
- implementing the project
- evaluating and reviewing the project
- disseminating information about the project and its outcomes.

The project life cycle and the tools and techniques associated with each stage are explored in Chapters 2 to 5.

What are the benefits of project management? The main benefits of using a people-centred approach to project management is that it is likely to motivate both the project team and other stakeholders to ensure that the project is successful. In addition, using an appropriate range of project management tools and techniques means that the project is more likely to be delivered on time and to the right standards. The project manager is likely to feel confident that the team has fully researched the project and produced a detailed project plan that is well grounded in reality. This includes having worked out the risks associated with the project and having made allowances for situations that might arise and disrupt progress. Project management also includes considering and developing contingency plans that may be put into practice relatively easily. This can ease the stress that some people feel when unexpected events occur.

In addition, the project management process produces 'hard' outcomes, including a range of documents (project brief, specifications, contracts, budgets), and this documentation can be used in lots of different situations including to communicate the project process to other ILS staff, to record key decisions, to enable staff who become involved in the project at a late stage to understand and follow the project process, and as a back-up in case of illness, holidays or other absences.

Why do projects go wrong?

Newspapers thrive on stories of project failure and examples include projects that have gone over budget by millions or over time by years, for example many public sector IT or building projects. Some projects result in the production of so-called 'white elephants' such as the Millennium Dome in London.

Puleo (2002) identifies some of the more common pitfalls of project management:

- lack of a project sponsor such as senior management or executive team
- lack of a steering committee to achieve co-ordination and collaboration among people across organizations
- the wrong project manager, i.e. someone without the necessary project management, motivational, leadership and change agent skills
- lack of dedicated team effort; team members are given insufficient time to carry out their project work
- lack of co-ordination between the organization's projects and everyday services.

One of the purposes of this book is to enable ILS project managers to lead successful projects and avoid the common problems outlined above.

Overview of the book's chapters

In this book project management is explored from a number of different perspectives. It is divided into three parts:

- Introduction
- The project life cycle, systems and processes
- Projects and people.

This chapter provides an introduction to project management and also the book.

Part 2, 'The project life cycle, systems and processes' is made up of Chapters 2–7. Chapter 2 introduces the project life cycle and then focuses on the important initial stages of a project, i.e. project analysis. It outlines the activities that take place at the start of a project including: initiation, initial research, identifying the project team, project structure, project communications, risk analysis, legal issues, producing a project brief and obtaining approval. It also covers legal issues such as employment, health and safety, data protection, intellectual property, etc.

Chapter 3 is concerned with planning the project and introduces a wide range of project management tools and techniques such as GANTT charts and PERT diagrams. The project planning process normally involves three stages: researching the project, detailed planning, and documenting and communicating the plan. This chapter also covers the effective management of project staff, resources and schedule.

Chapter 4 is concerned with implementing the project. This stage involves putting the plan into action and actually 'doing' the project and the project manager is likely to be involved in managing people, resources and the project process. The latter involves monitoring the project's progress and comparing it with the plan and, where appropriate, taking corrective action. Finally the project will be completed and the project manager needs to ensure that the project is closed: that all reports are written, loose ends are finished off and there is some formal or informal activity to close the project. This may range from tea and biscuits at a final team meeting through to a more formal celebration. The people side of projects, covered in detail in Part 3, is an essential concern for project managers.

Chapter 5 is concerned with project evaluation and dissemination. Evaluation of a project is important as it enables the project manager and others to identify their effectiveness, areas of strength and weakness, and lessons for the future. It is then important to disseminate the outcomes of the evaluation process to funders or sponsors of the project as well as the information and library community. This chapter introduces report writing and provides simple guidelines for writing project management reports. Project work often results in conference papers at professional meetings and also presentations, for example to the funding agency, the employer or professional groups. This topic is explored and guidelines are provided to enable project managers to identify and produce papers and presentations that are professional and communicate a clear message. In addition this chapter includes a brief overview of the use of websites as a means of disseminating project information.

The money side of projects is covered in Chapter 6. This is an important area as library and information workers are often involved in the bidding and tendering process, which involves knowing where to access external funds and how much money you may need to carry out the project. This is an important process as if you get it wrong then you may be unable to complete the project or you may have to subsidize it from another budget. Once you have obtained the finance required for the project then it is important to be able to keep records of how the money is spent and also to be able to produce the required financial reports. For example most agencies that provide project money have very strict reporting rules that require you clearly demonstrate at regular intervals, typically monthly or three-monthly, how you are spending the money. Finally, it is worthwhile thinking about the auditing process that will need to take place for you to demonstrate that you have fulfilled your contracts and spent the money in the agreed manner. This chapter is complemented by a glossary in Appendix A containing terms used in the world of accounting and finance.

Nowadays it is almost impossible to imagine managing a project without the use of information and communication technologies (ICT) and this topic is covered in Chapter 7 which is divided into three sections: virtual communications, project management software and other software. Virtual communication tools include e-mail, discussion or bulletin boards, chat or conference rooms, and videoconferencing and other tools.

While e-mail has been extensively used in ILS for many years the use of other virtual communication tools is becoming increasingly common. This chapter explores their advantages and disadvantages, and how they may be effectively used in team work. Project management software is an important tool for project managers, regularly used to plan the project, manage the information e.g. financial information, monitor the project, and to produce a range of printouts and reports. A wide range of project management packages are available and this chapter introduces MS Project, one of the most commonly used commercial packages, and also a range of free or low-cost shareware packages. The chapter also briefly evaluates the use of project management software by ILS workers.

Part 3 of the book is concerned with the people side of projects. The project manager needs to work with a wide range of people and the human side of projects is explored in Chapter 8. As project manager it is important to be able to create a positive team culture so that individual team members (whether conscripts or volunteers) are enthusiastic and motivated about working on the project. This chapter provides a brief theoretical framework to common ideas about teamwork and then explores particular issues, e.g. team development, team roles and managing challenging situations. Chapter 8 also explores managing international projects and working in multicultural teams, and this section is followed by an overview of virtual teamwork. The final section in this chapter is concerned with the management of change and it outlines a framework showing the common psychological processes associated with change and the different actions that a project manager may take to facilitate the change process.

The people side of projects continues to be explored in Chapter 9 which investigates working in partnership, for example with different professional groups, with workers from different organizations and also with user groups and volunteers. Many projects involve people from different professional backgrounds working together. This means that they are likely to hold different values and beliefs, and also have different working practices. An awareness of these and ways of managing the team to take into account these differences can be very important for the success of the project. This chapter provides some practical guidance for project managers on successful working in partnership.

Chapter 10 is concerned with the experiences of project workers and managers, and it explores three different perspectives: contract project workers, staff working on projects as part of their ILS role, and project managers. The chapter briefly reviews the rise of the contract ILS worker and identifies some of the issues that arise in this type of work including staff development, project closure and supporting yourself. In addition, the chapter considers the experiences of ILS staff who are asked to become involved in a project as part of their 'normal' roles and responsibilities. At a time when the majority of library and information workers have heavy workloads this can be a challenging situation and topics covered include balancing the project work and other responsibilities, working with a project manager and line manager, and working with colleagues not involved in the project.

The final section in this chapter is concerned with self-management, a subject relevant to both project workers and managers, and covers the following topics: the importance of goals and SMART outcomes, managing time, looking after yourself, gaining support e.g. through mentoring, and managing your career.

Chapter 11 focuses on the knowledge and skills required by project managers, and also training and education provision in this area. Finally, there is a list of printed and electronic resources on project management.

Reference

Puleo, L. (2002) Some of the More Common Pitfalls of Project Management, *Accounting Today*, www.electronicaccount.com/AccountingToday/.

Part 2

The project life cycle, systems and processes

2

The project life cycle and project analysis

Introduction

The purpose of this chapter is to introduce and outline the project life cycle, an indication of the types of processes a project manager will facilitate throughout the life of the project. Every project involves working through a distinct cycle, as shown in Figure 2.1.

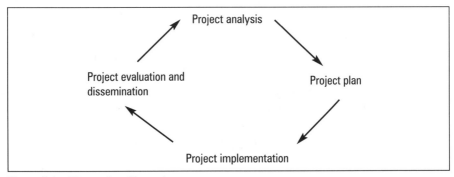

Figure 2.1   The project life cycle

Each of the project stages is made up of a series of activities as indicated below:

- Project analysis
  - project initiation
  - defining the project
  - risk analysis and management
  - legal issues
  - producing a project brief
  - gaining approval for the project
- Project plan
  - researching the project
  - developing the project plan
  - documenting and communicating the plan
- Project implementation
  - implementing the project
  - closing the project

- Project evaluation and dissemination
  — evaluating and reviewing the project
  — disseminating the project outcomes.

This chapter considers the first stage, i.e. the project analysis, and the following three chapters cover the subsequent stages.

Initiation

The idea for a project may originate in a number of different ways. Sometimes the project concept arises within a management or executive team who wish to steer their ILS in a particular direction. Some projects develop in response to government or local authority policies that are supported by specialist funds. Projects and other initiatives are often initiated by professional groups, for example the Consortium of University Research Libraries (CURL) or Research Support Libraries Programme (RSLP), or by national bodies such as the Joint Information Systems Committee (JISC) in response to changes in government policies or a desire to develop ILS systems and services at a national level in a particular direction.

Sometimes the basic idea behind the project is developed outside the ILS, perhaps as part of a strategic change within the parent organization, and the ILS staff are then asked to design and carry out the work, e.g. opening a new library or service. Or an information worker may attend a meeting or conference and come back to their ILS with a 'good idea' which then evolves into a project. Perhaps an information manager may want to extend their service and then find out that there is the possibility of gaining funding from an external body, so giving rise to a new project.

Example   Installation of an access control system in a university library

This example illustrates how a project arose in response to an in-house situation.

'The main library at Oxford Brookes University had become the target for local thieves. 165 thefts of personal property occurred between 1999 and 2001 and this despite the introduction in October 2000 of regular patrols by staff. Many users relaxed once in the library and tended to leave their bags unattended. Staff left leaflets warning users of the dangers but still the thefts continued. Staff began to feel increasingly uneasy about the situation. We all agreed that the worst aspect was dealing with upset and sometimes traumatized users. We felt responsible yet powerless to improve the situation. Staff working late in the evening and at weekends began to feel vulnerable too. Thames Valley police advised us that the only way of significantly reducing the level of theft would be to introduce some sort of access control system. The University responded to lobbying by Dr Helen Workman, Director of Learning Resources, and agreed to fund an access control system for the Headington Library but there would be no money available for extra staffing. This money was released in June 2001 and we could not justify delaying the implementation. If humanly possible we wanted this security in for week 0 of the autumn term.' (Hall, 2002, p.1)

Defining the project

Defining the project involves identifying the basic project idea (or vision) and what the project must achieve, i.e. the project outcomes. A vision is something that people will work towards and be motivated by. In an ideal world it inspires and captures the core values and beliefs of a team and enables the project manager to motivate team members to translate the vision into reality.

To turn a vision into a reality involves identifying the project objectives. These then need to be compared with the ILS's and the organization's objectives: if the project doesn't support these objectives it could then result in a diversion of staff time and resources from the main work of the ILS and its parent organization.

The scope of the project also needs to be identified. Many projects start off with a small-scope, pilot or research phase, and then, depending on the success of that, will expand. For example, the initial scope of a project on the design and development of multimedia-based learning materials was limited to the development of three basic resources. Once these had been produced and the project evaluated then the scope was broadened to another subject area. Sometimes a project will exclude some aspect of work and this needs to be clearly identified with the rationale behind this decision.

The timescale of the project needs to be considered too. What are the proposed start and end dates? How do these fit in with the ILS service requirements? What might be the impact of seasonal variations in the workload of the ILS? It is worthwhile identifying some project 'milestones': important landmarks in the project process. Two obvious milestones are the project start and end dates. In a project involving moving a library, milestones could include end of weeding of stock, end of changing catalogue records, all periodicals moved to new location, all books moved to new location. They are important as they can be real motivators to staff who can see how the progress is moving forward to its completion. Milestones provide useful measures for evaluating and celebrating the success of the project throughout the project process.

At the project-planning stage you will also need to consider the resourcing requirements of the project. At this stage, there is no need to carry out a detailed staffing or financial analysis but there does need to be some general indication of the staffing costs and also the financial costs of the project.

Initial research

The project analysis stage involves some initial research as you will need to think through your ideas, identify good practice and find out if other information and library workers are involved in similar projects. Time spent on this initial research will mean that you may be able to learn from good practice and the strengths and weaknesses of other projects. Useful sources of information include the professional literature, conferences and meetings, discussion lists and colleagues.

Working with different groups of people

A wide range of people are likely to be involved in your project and may be influenced by its implementation process and outcomes. This range includes information and library staff, stakeholders, allies and champions, project partners, project funders and the wider ILS profession. Each of these groups of people is considered below.

Information and library staff

In very small or simple projects the project may be carried out by one person, while in more complex and larger projects it may be a group of staff either in the same or different ILS. The scope for selecting team members is often limited in smaller ILS and while ideally the focus should be on identifying people with specific knowledge and skills, interest and enthusiasm for the project, in many situations we have no choice as to the selection of team members and the project manager may have to lead de-motivated or unenthusiastic staff.

Sometimes project managers are in the fortunate position of working with a group of highly motivated people and in this situation it is often useful to include a couple of members of staff who take on a 'critical friend' role. These people often provide a helpful counter-balance to the positive enthusiasts who don't always see potential problem areas. The people side of the project management process is considered in more depth in Chapter 8.

As project manager working on an in-house project you are likely to be working with two distinct groups of ILS staff: staff working on the project and those who aren't directly engaged in project work. As project manager it is important to ensure that the staff who are not actively engaged in the project are taken into consideration throughout the project. They need to be kept up to date about the project and its development. In addition this group of staff often keep the main services and systems of an ILS working throughout the life of the project and their work needs to be acknowledged and validated. This is particularly true in high-profile projects where 'fame and fortune' may be linked to the project workers while the staff who provided the backbone of the ILS service are in danger of becoming invisible. If this type of division arises it can lead to resentment and bad feeling between different groups of staff.

Many ILS project teams are set up by national or regional organizations such as the British Library, Resource and JISC. In these situations project teams are likely to be made up of ILS staff from a diverse range of organizations and they offer the opportunity to work collaboratively and network across organizational and/or sector boundaries. The management issues that arise in this situation are considered in Chapter 9.

Many projects employ short-term contract information workers and this situation is considered in Chapter 10. If your project employs contract staff then at the project analysis stage it is worthwhile considering the needs of these staff to ensure that they have access to the same performance management and staff development processes as do permanent staff. This is likely to include the following: induction, performance review or appraisal processes, staff development and mentoring (if there is a scheme within the ILS or employing organization).

Stakeholders

Whatever the size or complexity of the project there will be a relatively large number of people who have a specific interest and investment in the ILS, the project and its outcomes. These stakeholders may be located within or outside of your organization. They will include your customers, suppliers, sponsor, colleagues not involved in the project, colleagues from other sections of your organization and others. At an early stage in your project it is worthwhile spending some time identifying who are your stakeholders. You will also need to spend some time identifying and considering their needs and expectations from the project. The author's experience is that it is really well worthwhile investing time in building up relationships and creating effective communication channels with stakeholders. These are the people who are likely to be important allies and they can also cause major problems to a project if they are ignored.

Allies and champions

Allies and champions are people who will support and champion your project; they may be located within your organization or outside it. Identifying and getting to know people who will provide this type of support can be crucial as they will be able to give you and the project support. Identifying a champion at a senior level within your organization can be very useful as this is a person who will probably be willing to 'fight your corner' at meetings from which you may be excluded, for example senior management meetings. Spending a little time identifying and building up your relationship with allies and champions will tend to pay dividends if the going gets hard.

Project partners

Nowadays many projects are carried out in partnership with colleagues from other ILS or other professional groups. The issue of partnership working is considered so important that it is covered in a separate chapter, Chapter 9.

Project funders

Chapter 6 considers the process of bidding for funds from a diverse range of organizations and trusts. As a project manager it is worthwhile considering the staff with whom you work in the funding organization as important players in your team. Spending time getting to know these people and their requirements is well worthwhile.

The wider ILS profession

At any time your project is likely to be one of many taking place within the regional, national and international ILS communities. These communities offer a wealth of information and support, and your project work may result in outcomes that can be used by project workers around the world. Active participation in online networks offers a simple and cheap approach to exchanging information and exploring ideas; this is considered in Chapter 7. In contrast conferences and networking meetings are often used to disseminate project findings and this is considered in Chapter 5.

Management structure

It is important to think about how you are going to manage the project and the systems and structures you need in place to support both you as project manager and also the project. This will depend on the size and complexity of your project.

If you are working on a large or complex one then it is well worthwhile involving at least three different groups of staff in the project process: a steering group, the management group and the project team. The project manager will be a member of all three groups and individual project team members, e.g. people with a particular expertise, may also be members of the management team. This is illustrated in Figure 2.2.

The purpose of the steering group is to provide general guidance and 'a steer' to the project. Such a group is often an important way of involving a range of stakeholders in the project and it is likely to be made up of 'the great and the good'. If you are involved in setting one up it is worthwhile thinking about the types of expertise and support that you will find helpful to the project. Ideally the steering

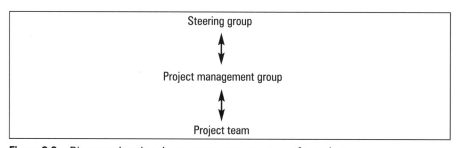

Figure 2.2   Diagram showing the management structure of a project

group will include a number of different stakeholders and also people who will champion the project in a number of different arenas.

> A well constituted steering or advisory group brings together key players who will be influential in decision-making about future choices relating to short-term project outputs as well as being well-positioned to shape the conditions for the likely future uptake of products or services and their embedding in organisational or disciplinary contexts. Steering group members are potentially effective in networking with a broader set of actors, so facilitating transfer of knowledge, know-how and exploitable products into other settings. . . . Broadly based steering groups . . . will be representative of the different stakeholder interests and perspectives . . . which may well be conflictual or in some degree of tension. These differences or tensions are generally reproduced within the innovation itself, unless addressed at a higher level. Steering groups are an appropriate forum for exploring real and imagined differences, for optimising potential outcomes for the different parties, and for engaging with the wider issues that are raised by developments.
>
> (Kelleher, Sommerlad and Stern, 1996)

The management group will be made up of people who are involved in the project at a senior level and their role is to identify strategy and enable it to be put into action. This group is particularly important if there are significant problems to resolve. As project manager you will find it very useful to have a group of senior staff who will provide you with support and who may be used to confirm any difficult decisions that you need to make.

In contrast the project team will be the operational team and made up of project workers. Their role is to make the project happen, resolve the problems and report to the management team. It is not mandatory to have three groups and, in small projects, the steering group and the management group may be merged into one.

Example   Management of a project for moving a library into a new building

Allen and Bowden (2001, p.13) describe the project management process for the movement of the Dublin City University 's library's 250,000-print stock into a new building (DCU). This process involved the establishment of an appropriate committee as follows:

> 'From the planning stage, a sub-librarian (Planning & Development) was appointed. Subcommittees were then formed to plan, co-ordinate and implement the transfer of resources and services from the old to the new library building. The challenge facing the subcommittee involved in the transfer of stock was the logistics of moving the library's print stock by the

stated deadline, while maintaining, as far as possible, a full service. Methods used by other libraries were investigated and whilst they all had merits, it was decided that a unique system, tailored to DCU Library's needs, was required. To meet the challenge, the subcommittee devised the work in two phases, the pre-move planning and the actual move. Broad objectives were set for each phase. In phase one, a stock measurement process and coding system was developed to facilitate the integration and distribution of books and journals to the four-storey building. In phase two, a system for the physical movement of the library's print collections was identified.'

Although many information and library projects are managed through formal committees and meetings there are other less formal approaches to project management as shown in the following example:

Example   Installation of an access control system in a university library

'Here at Brookes some of us are not big on project teams and what are those gatherings called, oh yes, meetings . . . SURELY WE MUST HAVE HAD ONE MEETING? Yes, on D-day minus 13 we all sat down together with SB Electronics to discuss the minutiae of how the system worked. From these discussions procedures for visitors and staff and students who forgot their cards evolved. We knew what we wanted but needed to understand how the system would allow us to achieve it.' (Hall, 2002)

This doesn't mean that there wasn't a lot of communication taking place and it is clear that different people were involved in different aspects of the project and helped to ensure that it was successful, e.g. 'Tony kept an eagle eye on proceedings and ensured that each party talked to the other'.

Many ILS projects are small ones and don't need a complex management structure. However even if you are project manager and project team rolled into one, it is worthwhile thinking about how you will gain support for your project activities and report on them.

Many funding organizations will require that the project is managed and governed in a particular way, for example through a series of steering groups, interest groups or committees. Typically the sponsor may require the involvement of a steering committee and a management committee. This enables them to be satisfied that the project will be well managed and also that themselves and other stakeholders will have an opportunity to influence the direction of the project. In some situations the management and governance structure may be quite complex, as demonstrated in the JISC example below, or unusual project management structures may be created to deal with a particular situation as shown in the SPP example.

Example   JISC Information Environment Development Programmes

The JISC website provides much detailed information about the ways in which JISC structures and manages projects, e.g. the Information Environment Development Programme is made up of a series of projects and staff working on an individual project may be involved in up to six committees or groups as follows:

- JISC Executive
- Joint Committee Information Environment (JCIE)
- programme level advisory boards
- project clusters
- project advisory groups
- local project groups.

The JISC website (www.jisc.ac.uk) indicates the different roles and responsibilities of these different groups.

Example   Subject Portal Project: an unusual project structure

Ruth Martin (2003, p.53) reports on a project to transform the subject hubs of the Resource Discovery Network (RDN) into portals. The Subject Portals Project (SPP) is supported by JISC funding and she describes the project management structure as follows:

> 'The overall co-ordination of tasks has been the responsibility of a project manager based at the Ukoln research centre at the University of Bath . . . while the technical co-ordination has been managed by Jasper Tredgold of the ILRT at the University of Bristol. We have two private websites and two team mailing lists just to handle the internal communication. At times keeping it all together has felt like standing up to conduct a symphony orchestra, but it has provided a marked success. In fact, we have been asked by JISC's Quality Assurance Focus to write a case study of the SPP's project management to act as guidance on best practice for other projects.'

Different types of team work

At the start of a project it is worthwhile thinking about the type of team work that is required within a project. Different types of project are best managed by organizing and managing teams in different ways.

Traditional ILS work involves working in 'process' teams where people undertake routine and standardized activities or tasks. This is the most common form of work and it has the following features:

- It is predictable.
- It repeats.

- It is standardized.
- It takes place over a predictable time period.
- It maintains the status quo.

In contrast project work is the exact opposite. It has the following features:

- It is unpredictable.
- It is unique.
- It may be difficult to standardize.
- It takes place over an estimated time period.
- It results in change.

This means that project teams need to be managed in a different way to process teams. To complicate matters further there are different types of project work and they may involve individuals (or sub-groups) working independently, co-operatively or collaboratively. The differences between these types of work are outlined in Table 2.1. As project manager it is worthwhile spending some time thinking about the best type of approach to project work for your team.

Table 2.1 Different types of team work

	Independent	**Co-operative**	**Collaborative**
Definition	Individuals work by themselves on their own tasks. They each have their own goal.	A task is divided into sections and individuals are responsible for their own piece of work. They each have their own goal.	The team works together on the task. They are working towards a shared goal.
Types of tasks	Organizing room bookings. Acting as a contact person.	Writing a project report.	Producing a project plan. Writing a project report.
Effective management patterns	Individuals are briefed and deadlines are agreed. Individuals report back to project manager and/or team meetings.	The whole team is briefed and deadlines are agreed. Division of work is agreed. Boundaries between tasks are clarified. Individuals agree how they will communicate with each other and deal with critical or unexpected circumstances.	The whole team is briefed and deadlines are agreed. Division of work is agreed. Individuals discuss and agree how they will work with each other. Future meeting dates are set for collaborative work to take place.

Sometimes project managers will assume that their project team will work either co-operatively or collaboratively when their specific project is best suited by individual types of work. This is demonstrated in the following example:

Example   Choosing types of team work

The author was running a workshop on team building and one of the delegates outlined the problems that he was experiencing within his workplace library. He was involved in leading a retrospective cataloguing project and found it difficult to get staff to attend project meetings and contribute to them. He said, 'All they want to do is get on with the work and they hate coming to meetings'. After some discussion it became clear that the team members were all working extremely effectively on their allocated tasks and reported directly back to their project manager. There was no real need for them to meet with each other and discuss their progress although in reality this tended to happen informally over the photocopier. The project manager was attempting to lead team meetings when they weren't really required. Once he had explored the different patterns of team working within a project then he realized that it was probably most effective to manage the individuals rather than attempt to lead the project via team meetings.

Project communications

A common feature of successful projects is that the project communication process has been thought through and planned in some detail. At the project analysis stage it is worthwhile thinking about how this communication process is going to be managed. This involves thinking in broad terms about the answers to the following questions:

- Who will be working on the project?
- Who will be affected by the project?
- When do we need to communicate?
- Who is responsible for implementing the communications strategy?
- With whom will you communicate?
- What will you communicate?
- How you will communicate?
- What channels are required for feedback?
- Who is responsible for giving, receiving and acting on feedback?

Information and advice on the use of reports, presentations and websites in disseminating information about the project is given in Chapter 5. Information on the use of electronic communications, i.e. e-mail, discussion lists, bulletin boards, conference or chat rooms and videoconferencing, is considered in Chapter 7.

Risk analysis and management

The time to start thinking about what might go wrong in the project is at the very start. Risk analysis involves identifying events or situations that may cause the project to fail and then managing them to ensure that the project is successful. There are four main types of risks:

- Technical risks, e.g. new software system doesn't work.
- Financial risks, e.g. sponsor withdraws or reduces support.
- Process risks, e.g. failure of project plan, poor team performance, illness of key members of staff.

- External risks occurring when a change in the external environment affects project outcomes, e.g. takeover of company, major fluctuations in exchange rates, terrorist attacks.

Risk management involves identifying potential risks and then estimating their probability. This is illustrated in Tables 2.2 and 2.3.

Project management tools provide a quantitative method of assessing and ranking risks. The following procedure is adapted from Young (1998):

1 Identify a list of potential risks.
2 Assess the probability of the occurrence of each risk as follows:
   a High probability – this situation is highly likely to occur (>80% probability).
   b Medium – there is an average probability that this will occur (20–80% probability).
   c Low – this situation is unlikely to occur (<20% probability).
3 Assess the impact on the project if it does happen:
   a High – serious impact on project, e.g. will result in project not meeting schedule or budget, or adverse effects on customers.
   b Medium – less serious impact on project, e.g. may affect budget, minor adverse effects on staff.
   c Low – minimum effect on project and its outcomes.
4 Identify potential impact on project by ranking risks using the information presented in Table 2.4.
5 Once the potential risks have been assessed and ranked then they can be managed in the following way:
   a Unacceptable risks – these need to be eliminated from the project. These types of risks need to be considered as serious issues by the project steering and management teams.
   b High risks – these need to be taken into account in the project-planning process. Contingency plans must be created to help deal with these risks. These risks need to be carefully monitored and reviewed at each project, management and steering group meeting.
   c Medium risks – these risks need to be carefully monitored and reviewed at each project meeting.
   d Low risks – these risks need to be carefully monitored and reviewed at each project meeting.

It is worth highlighting that this risk analysis process is a subjective one and only as good as the estimates of the project team and manager. If you are involved in carrying out this type of process in practice then it is worthwhile ensuring that your team includes people willing to take both an optimistic and pessimistic perspective as this will help you to carry out a balanced risk assessment.

Table 2.2 Risk assessment: implementing a new ICT system

Potential risks	How serious a threat is it to the project?	What is the probability of this happening?	What could be done to manage the potential threat?
Project manager is off sick for more than five working days.	Very serious. Project manager is main driver and lynch pin of project.	Low probability. Project manager has only had three days' sick leave in past five years.	Ensure that there is an assistant project manager (this offers a good staff development opportunity). Ensure that project files and records are accessible.
Delay in supply of new hardware.	Very serious. This would delay project.	Low probability. Supplier able to demonstrate achievement of delivery dates.	Build in slack at this stage of project. Write in delivery times into contract. Use supplier with an excellent track record.
Delay in recruitment of project team.	Very serious. This would delay the project.	High probability. Recruitment and selection process within ILS is traditionally slow. Also dependent on attracting suitable candidates.	Build slack into project plan. Discuss with human resources director and gain support for a speedy recruitment process. Raise as issue with steering group.
Re-cataloguing not up to required standard.	Very serious. This would adversely affect quality of product.	Low probability. Project is using experienced staff who have demonstrated their skills in previous projects.	Set up standard quality procedures.

Table 2.3 Risk assessment: implementing an online project

Risk	Likelihood	Consequences	Contingency
Single module is not completed on schedule.	High – possible.	Must provide an alternative programme.	Enlist additional assistance.
Impossible to overcome technical snags.	High – possible.	Website facilities are limited. Risk of looking old-fashioned and not meeting all specification requirements.	Explore alternative methods of delivery using proven technology.
Major problems thrown up in online pilot.	Medium – plausible.	Website not ready on time owing to need to rewrite and sort out technical snags.	Test everything as project develops. Make sure website is well tested before pilot.
Student enrolment is low.	Medium – plausible.	Website is under-used in next academic year.	Target lecturers/ departments to ensure positive take up of website. Project manager to get involved in induction events and advertise website.
Member of project team leaves.	Medium/low – possible.	Don't complete website on time.	Identify back-up staff, e.g. freelance developers.
Alternative commercial product becomes available.	Low – plausible.	Redundant product.	Assess commercial product for adoption.

This example is adapted from Peacock, J. (2002) *Project Strategy Plan: AIRS Online*, www.library.qut.edu.au/infoliteracy/projects current/

Table 2.4 Risk assessment

Probability	Impact on project		
	Low	Medium	High
High	Medium – significant but not expected to affect milestones or project outcomes.	High – major impact on project. May result in project not reaching milestones or outcomes.	Unacceptable – these will result in project failure.
Medium	Low – not expected to have a serious impact on the project.	High – major impact on project. May result in project not reaching milestones or outcomes.	Unacceptable – these will result in project failure.
Low	Low – not expected to have aserious impact on the project.	Medium – significant but not expected to affect milestones or project outcomes.	High – major impact on project. May result in project not reaching milestones or outcomes.

Legal issues

A large number of legal issues may arise during project work and the purpose of this section is to indicate some of the areas that you will need to consider. If you are involved in setting up a new project within your organization then it is worthwhile talking to the relevant experts, e.g. human resources director, health and safety officer, very early in the project's life.

This section focuses on employment legislation, health and safety, data protection and copyright in the UK. A number of books provide excellent advice on a wider range of legal issues for information professionals, including Pedley (2003) and Armstrong and Bebbington (2003).

Employment

If you employ individuals on your project then you will have to comply with national and European legislation on employment. This means taking into account legislation such as:

- Equal Pay Act 1970
- Sex Discrimination Act 1975
- Race Relations Act 1976
- Disability Discrimination Act 1995
- Employment Rights Act 1996
- Working Time Regulations 1998
- Gender Reassignment Regulations 1999
- Employment Relations Act 1999
- Employment Act 2002

- Fixed-Term Employees (Prevention of Less Favourable Treatment) Regulations 2002
- Part-Time Workers (Prevention of Less Favourable Treatment) Regulations 2002 and (Amendment) Regulations 2002.

It is beyond the scope of this book to provide detailed guidance on the formal aspects of employment and employment legislation. The main message for project managers is to ensure that you obtain good-quality advice from a qualified human resource manager. In the UK the professional association for human resource managers is the Chartered Institute for Personnel and Development (CIPD); www.cipd.org.uk.

In some (hopefully very rare) instances project managers may become involved in managing difficult situations such as short- and long-term absenteeism, poor performance, e-mail or internet abuse, alcohol or drug abuse, too much stress, misconduct in work, misconduct outside work, or vicarious liability. In these types of situations the general advice is to obtain specialist advice from the employing organization's human resource manager as soon as the problem is identified. The human resource manager will advise you on how to manage the situation, the organizational procedure for dealing with it, and also how to document the issue. In all of these kinds of situations it is vitally important that correct procedures are followed; otherwise they may become extremely difficult and time consuming to manage.

Health and safety

Health and safety at work is about preventing people from being harmed by taking the right precautions and providing a satisfactory work environment. In the UK, legislation covering health and safety at work includes:

- Health and Safety at Work Act 1974
- Management of Health and Safety at Work Regulations 1992
- Health and Safety (Consultation with Employees) Regulations 1996
- Safety Representatives and Safety Committees Regulations 1977.

In the UK, the Health and Safety Executive (HSE) and local authorities administer these laws. You can find out more about health and safety at work by contacting your health and safety officer or the HSE at www.hse.gov.uk or 01787 881165.

There are many common risks at work and typical examples relevant to information and library work include slips, trips and falls; hazardous substances; lifting and carrying; repetitive movements; noise; vibration; electricity; work equipment; maintenance and building work; and fire, explosion or radiation. At the start of any project it is important to think about the health and safety implications and to carry out a risk assessment. The first person to contact is your health and safety officer who will either carry out the risk assessment or show you how to complete one. Once the risk assessment has been completed it is important to follow up any actions.

Example Health and safety during a library move

The author was involved in the movement of an academic library into a new building. In addition to the permanent staff, 17 temporary 'movers and shifters' were employed to carry out much of the manual work. Just before the move began, all the permanent staff were given a refresher course on lifting and moving by the health and safety officer. On their first day of employment in the library all the temporary staff were given a half-day course on lifting and moving and this was also run by the university's health and safety officer. These courses were carefully documented and everyone was expected to sign an attendance sheet both at the start and end of the course. The course outline and all teaching materials were retained by the project team too. On the second day of employment one of the temporary staff damaged a foot and, as a result, attempted to sue the university. After a long-drawn-out process which was managed by the university's solicitor the case was dropped as the project manager and university were able to demonstrate that they had taken appropriate action, well documented through the training course, to inform both temporary and permanent staff on good practice in manual handling and that the person in question had 'broken the rules'.

Data protection

Data protection is concerned with personal data held in electronic or printed format. Relevant legislation covering this topic includes:

- Data Protection Act 1998
- Human Rights Act 1998
- Freedom of Information Act 2000
- Regulation of Investigatory Powers Act 2000
- Telecommunications (Lawful Business Practice) (Interception of Communications) Regulations 2000.

In the UK further information about data protection is available from www. dataprotection.gov.uk. This site outlines the principles of good practice in data protection as follows:

Anyone processing personal data must comply with the eight enforceable principles of good practice. Data must be:

- fairly and lawfully processed;
- processed for limited purposes;
- adequate, relevant and not excessive;
- accurate;
- not kept longer than necessary;
- processed in accordance with the data subject's rights;

- secure;
- not transferred to countries without adequate protection.

Personal data covers both facts and opinions about the individual. It also includes information regarding the intentions of the data controller towards the individual, although in some limited circumstances exemptions will apply. With processing, the definition is far wider than before. For example, it incorporates the concepts of 'obtaining', 'holding' and 'disclosing'.

Copyright

While it is really important that projects don't accidentally or intentionally infringe copyright legislation, this is a complex issue. There are some very good guides to copyright legislation available, for example on the JISC website (www.jisc.ac.uk) and that written by Norman (2003).

Many projects result in the development of printed or electronic publications, websites or other materials and these may contain text, images or audiovisual materials such as video clips and audio tapes. It is vitally important to obtain written permission if you are using other people's intellectual property, e.g. images, text, sound, animation, list of URLs. Key points to cover when writing for permission include:

- a bibliographic reference for the required material
- a list of the pages, screens and frames
- details of material in preparation: outline materials, audience, size of audience, proposed usage (e.g. three times per year), life span (e.g. two years), proposed use (e.g. educational, not-for-profit, commercial)
- details of the organization (e.g. public, private or third sector).

Many projects appoint one person as copyright officer and their role includes advising project members on copyright issues, ensuring that copyright clearance is obtained for all relevant items and maintaining appropriate records.

Producing a project brief

As a result of your informal discussions and initial research you will find that you can produce a project brief. As the name suggests, this is a short document (no more than two sides of A4) that outlines the proposed project. The project brief will answer the following questions:

- Why is the project important to the ILS?
- What are the project outcomes?
- What will it cost (staff time and resources)?
- Who will be involved in the project?

- When will it take place?
- What are the risks involved in the project?

The project brief serves a number of different purposes. The process of writing the brief helps to focus the mind and will start the process of moving from 'a good idea' to a project plan. The project brief may also be used as a discussion document in meetings where you are trying to obtain a decision to approve the project. It may additionally be used as a briefing document at the first project meeting and as a communication tool for other staff both within the ILS and across the wider organization. The project brief will form the basis of a range of other documents e.g. marketing, website information, annual report.

The written project brief is likely to be presented using the following types of headings:

- title of project
- aim of project
- main project outcomes
- rationale for project
- project stakeholders and how they will benefit from the project
- the scale of the project: time period, number of staff, resource requirements
- project milestones (key stages in the project process)
- potential risks and how they may be managed
- proposed project team
- relationship between this project and other projects.

The actual content of the project brief varies from project to project and organization to organization. Before you start writing yours it is worthwhile finding out if your ILS or organization has a standard template. Below is an example of the headings used in a project brief.

Example   Project brief or strategy plan

1. Management Summary
2. Introduction
3. Project aims and objectives
4. Project scope
5. Stakeholders
6. Resource assessment – resources required for the project or for each phase
7. Risk analysis
8. Outline of costs and benefits [omitted]
9. Project Management approach
10. Marketing and Communications strategy
11. Timelines and Milestones (Peacock 2002).

Once you have produced a project brief then it is important to identify what needs to happen next. Depending on the type of project and its context this may involve obtaining the go-ahead from senior managers and also negotiating and gaining access to the necessary staff resource and finance. Financing a project is considered in Chapter 6 while the people side of projects is considered in Chapters 8–11.

Obtaining approval for the project

Once you have analysed the situation and identified a potential project then the next stage is to obtain approval for the project. In the case of small-scale local projects this may involve obtaining approval from a manager or director. In large-scale projects involving a number of different organizations you may need to go through a relatively long approval process. If you are involved in bidding for funding for a project then it may need to go through an internal approval process followed by the submission of a competitive bid or tender (covered in Chapter 6).

Whatever the approval process, it is important to gain approval, ideally in writing or by e-mail, before you start the detailed planning of the project. Otherwise you may find that investing a lot of time and effort in detailed planning is wasted if approval is not given for the project. The next chapter outlines the project-planning process.

Summary

The project life cycle presents a framework outlining the different stages of a project. The first stage is the project initiation, which involves identifying the basic project idea and outlining the scope of the project: the desired outcomes, the likely timescale, who will be involved and what it is likely to cost. In addition the project manager needs to carry out research so that she or he is up to date with current practice in the topic of the project both in the context of the ILS profession and also in the wider world of organizational working. The analysis stage involves identifying the people who are likely to be involved in the project and the appropriate type of project team work, thinking about the management structure required to support it, defining the project and completing a risk analysis. Legal issues relating to employment, health and safety, copyright and data protection need to be considered at this stage too. The outcome of the analysis is a project brief; this is used for a variety of purposes including gaining approval for the project.

References

Allen, J. and Bowden, L. (2001) Move Over: moving DCU library's print material to the new library building, *SCONUL Newsletter*, **24**, (Winter), 13–16, www.sconul.ac.uk.

Armstrong, C. J. and Bebbington, L. W. (2003) *Staying Legal: a guide to issues and practice affecting the library, information and publishing sectors*, 2nd edn, London, Facet Publishing.

Hall, F. (2002) How to Install an Access Control System in less than 4 Months and Live to Tell the Tale, *SCONUL Newsletter*, **25**, (Spring), 87–9, www.sconul.ac.uk.

Kelleher, J., Sommerlad, E. and Stern, E. (1996) *Evaluation of the Electronic Libraries Programme. Guidelines for eLib project evaluation*, The Tavistock Institute, www.ukoln.ac.uk/services/elib/papers/tavistock/evaluation-guide/.

Martin, R. (2003) Turning Gateways into Portals, *Library & Information Update*, **2** (6), 52–3.

Norman, S. (2003) *Practical Copyright for Information Professionals: the CILIP handbook*, London, Facet Publishing.

Peacock, J. (2002) Project Strategy Plan, *AIRS-Online*, www.library.qut.edu.au/infoliteracy/projects.

Pedley, P. (2003) *Essential Law for Information Professionals*, London, Facet Publishing.

Young, T. L. (1998) *The Handbook of Project Management*, London, Kogan Page.

3

Planning the project

Introduction

The purpose of this chapter is to introduce the project planning process and to highlight the importance of planning to successful project management. Project planning involves researching the project, thinking ahead and identifying what needs to be done, the people who will carry out the work and the cost. In addition it involves identifying potential problems and developing contingency plans.

The structure of this chapter is based around the three stages of the project planning process: researching the project, detailed planning, and finally documenting and communicating the plan.

Researching the project

Researching the project involves both an external and internal analysis of the project environment. The external environment will help you to identify relevant political, economic or social factors that may have an impact on your project. In addition it will enable you to identify and learn from current good practice within the library and information profession. Information practitioners have extensive experience in a wide range of projects and, in general, they are very willing to share it. Sources of general information and advice include professional literature, conferences, networks and individual practitioners. E-mail discussion lists provide an important source of practical help and advice and these are considered in Chapter 7. Visits are often a useful way of finding out how other practitioners have tackled the same situation as shown in the following example.

Example Installation of an access control system in a university library

The following quotation demonstrates the value of taking time to visit other ILS that have tackled a similar project to your own.

'Linda Dixon, the Lending Services Librarian, organized two visits, one to the Economics Library at Oxford University and the other to Salford University. These visits were vital to our understanding of how the whole system would work and began to answer some of our questions relating to staffing, integration with our LMS and procedures for visitors. Although the Economics Library is a much smaller operation the principles behind the system are the same and it was extremely useful to see it working and hear from the staff how easy it was to operate. Knowing that we had no extra money for staffing this area obviously concerned us. Salford had tried recruiting staff specifically to operate the system but had found this unworkable and changed to using circulation staff. Salford stressed that staff needed to be able to deal well with users and understand the system and procedures associated with it. It was clear that some staff enjoyed the work and others were not so keen. A constant irritant was the number of forgotten cards by staff and students. Salford let us crawl all over their system and answered our numerous questions. We felt much better prepared for the work ahead as we sat on the train chugging back towards Oxford.' (Hall, 2002, pp.87–8)

The internal analysis involves identifying people, facilities, systems or services or ICT within your organization that may be used to help support the project. In addition this analysis may mean that you identify some potential blockages or challenges to your project. For example an internal analysis for a project in information skills teaching in a college found out that the two heads of department who were most likely to support and positively champion the proposed project were planning to leave the college at the end of the academic year. This information meant that the project team adapted their plan and changed the staffing of their steering and management teams to take into account this situation. This internal analysis often results in identifying individuals or teams who have specialist information or expertise that may be called on during the project.

Planning the project process

How is the project going to be managed and supported? The answer to this question really depends on the size of the project and its context. As mentioned in the previous chapter, if you are involved in major projects, i.e. large and complex projects that operate at a strategic level, then you may want to consider establishing a formal project management structure that involves different groups such as a:

- steering group
- management group
- project team.

This topic is discussed in more detail in Chapter 2.

Initial meetings

The purpose of the initial meeting is to get the project off to a good start. The activities that will take place in this meeting are likely to involve building relationships, outlining and determining the project parameters and also identifying an action plan (see Figure 3.1). The people side of this meeting is considered in more detail in Chapter 8 and, in the context of partnership working, in Chapter 9.

As project manager how will you address the following questions and issues at the initial project team meeting?

Why are we here?
Individual expectations
Employer expectations
Project leader expectations
Sponsor expectations

What are we here for?
The vision, mission, goal(s) and outcomes

Where are we going?
Actions, resources and timescales

How will we get there?
Use of project management tools
Internal and external communication strategies
Working practices
Review processes
Milestones and outcomes

What are our training and development needs?
Individual and team training and development needs

How will we look after ourselves?
Potential time management issues
Sources of support for individual team members e.g. by a mentor and/or line manager

Who will support the project?
Champions
Other supporters

What strategies will we use if things go wrong?

Figure 3.1 Checklist for the initial project team meeting

A typical agenda for the initial project is likely to cover the following topics.

Example **Initial project meeting agenda**

Introductions
The project brief
Areas of concern: hopes, fears and expectations
Project aims, outcomes and milestones

Project management and governance
Project team: roles and responsibilities
Project processes: ground rules and working practices
Other questions and answers
Outline action plan

Developing a project communication strategy

The advantage of establishing and managing the project communications is that you are able to manage the information flow and use this to support the project and everyone involved in it. The communication strategy needs to take into account both internal and external communications. The internal communications are those within the project team while the external communications are those between the project and all the stakeholders, i.e. customers, colleagues not involved in the project, suppliers, the library and information profession.

Internal communications

Internal communications within the project team are likely to take place through such mediums as meetings, e-mails, phone calls and a website. As project manager and team you need to decide your communication strategy and this is likely to include considering the answers to the following questions:

- Who has overall responsibility for monitoring and managing the communication process?
- Who will act as information manager for the communication process and provide archives, summaries, etc?
- When do you need to communicate?
- What will you communicate?
- How you will communicate – private e-mail, closed e-mail discussion list, website (including discussion boards and chat rooms), meetings?
- How often is everyone expected to communicate with each other?
- How will you handle annual leave or other absences?

External communications

How will the project manager and team communicate their work to people beyond the project team? The external communication process is a vital part of the project process and it involves managing the information and communication process with all the stakeholders. Ideally stakeholders should be kept informed about the project from start to finish so that they don't receive any unexpected shocks or surprises.

The amount of time and energy that is put into the external communications will depend on the nature of the project. In major projects the project team may have a working party whose primary consideration is the external communication process. The development of a strategy will help to ensure that all aspects of external communications are considered in some detail and this involves identifying:

- What is the purpose of the external communication strategy?
- Who is responsible for implementing the external communications strategy?
- Who will be working on the project?
- Who will be affected by the project?
- When do you need to communicate?
- With whom will you communicate?
- What will you communicate?
- How you will communicate – e-mail, website, press releases, leaflets and posters, briefing meetings?
- How will you obtain feedback about the project and its impact?
- Who is responsible for giving, receiving and acting on feedback?

It is worthwhile working through these questions with the project team and using your answers to develop an external communication strategy. In general, you will need to use as many different forms of communication as possible and this is likely to include meetings, presentations, workshops, briefings, press releases, e-mails, newsletters, posters, memos, letters and reports. You will also need to repeat your message a number of times over the time period of the project.

Example The implementation of an automated telephone renewals service at Northumbria University Library

In this project the team identified the importance of publicity and used a diverse range of methods to inform their stakeholders about the project and new service. Methods used included:

- printing of renewals number on the reverse of the university smartcard which is issued to all users
- insert in wallet given to everyone with their smartcard
- articles in university staff newsletter
- having academic representatives on the library users' panel
- printing of renewals number on book labels
- information on plasma screen at the largest campus which is used to promote services to users
- posters in key locations
- including information in relevant handouts and leaflets, e.g. .services for distance learners
- bookmark given out at loans desk

- callers to previous renewals numbers being advised of new telephone number and extended availability of service
- information on library web pages (Thompson, 2003, pp.25–6).

Example   Moving into a new building

A university library was moving to a new building during a summer vacation. The project team carried out an exercise that involved identifying the stakeholders in the move and their needs and expectations. This activity highlighted the needs of more than 100 students who were required to resit their examinations at the end of the vacation. As a result the project team gave one member of library staff responsibility for supporting these students. She wrote to each of them to explain what was happening over the summer and set up special arrangements so that they could have access to the materials that they needed for their studies. She acted as a personal contact point for these students. In the evaluation of the move these students praised the efforts of this librarian in helping them to successfully use the library resources over the summer period. One student wrote:

'Having a named contact was very helpful. I contacted her once by e-mail and she sorted out the books I needed. This was a very stressful time for me. If I failed my resit exams then I would have been chucked off the course. Sally helped reassure me that I would have access to the books I needed when I returned to uni for revision.'

Developing the project schedule

A key task for any project manager and team is to develop the project schedule. This outlines who does what, where and when. It is a crucial document and, once approved, provides a detailed plan for everyone working on the project. The project schedule may be written collaboratively by the project manager and team and will then need to be approved by the management group and steering group (if there is one). Sometimes this approval process involves a series of re-iterations before all the stakeholders are able to accept the schedule. The author's advice is to produce the project schedule as a collaborative piece of work between the manager and team workers as this means that it is more likely to encompass a wide range of ideas and experiences, and it will be owned by everyone involved in its production and implementation.

The starting point for the project schedule is the project brief and it is worth while re-reading this and, if necessary, clarifying the project's aims and outcomes. The next stage is to work out what needs to be done.

Overview of the project

At the start of a new project the size of the project and its complexity may make it appear to be a daunting process. Breaking the project down into manageable-sized pieces of work, each of which may be carried out by an individual or small team, is a simple way of organizing the work. Planning a project involves breaking it down into a series of stages and then within the stages breaking it down into manageable-sized tasks. This is illustrated in Figure 3.2 which shows a project that is divided into three stages. Each stage will be divided into a series of tasks and this is illustrated in Stage 2 which is divided into four tasks; then the first task is divided into four different activities.

Working through the project in this way means that it breaks down into extremely manageable pieces of work. The number of tasks and activities will depend on the size of the project; very complex projects may result in hundreds of tasks. The project team will have to decide on which level of detail they need to be focusing, i.e. how much detail the plan needs to contain. Individuals may be responsible for a stage, a task or an activity. In complex projects, for example those that involve collaborative working with information and library workers in different ILS, town or cities, regions or countries then this approach offers a means of dividing up the project. Individuals may work as a collaborative team on a particular stage, task or activity.

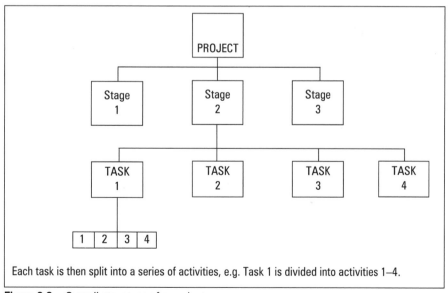

Each task is then split into a series of activities, e.g. Task 1 is divided into activities 1–4.

Figure 3.2 Overall structure of a project

Analysing tasks

For all types of projects it is important to analyse the work content of the project and this involves the following processes:

- identification of tasks with specific outcomes
- identification of recurrent tasks
- identification of milestones.

The specific outcomes of the project are best identified as SMART outcomes where the acronym SMART stands for Specific, Measurable, Achievable, Realistic, Timebound. SMART objectives are:

- Specific – they describe a specific activity.
- Measurable – it is possible to measure or identify when they are complete. There will be something tangible to see or hear.
- Achievable – it is possible to achieve the objective. You are not being asked to achieve an impossible task, e.g. one that involves a new invention.
- Realistic – it is possible to achieve the objective with the resources that are available and in the time required.
- Timebound – there is either a deadline or a set amount of time will be given to the activity, e.g. an hour a week.

Example   SMART Outcome

An example of a SMART outcome when moving a library of 100,000 items over a three month period was:

To move 100,000 items from their old to their new location and to have every book in the correct location with catalogue amendments by 1 September 2000.

A simple and practical way of analysing the work content is to ask the team members to identify the specific tasks that will need to take place for the project to be completed. You need to think about what level of detail to work at, as if you work out the schedule at too detailed a level you may be overwhelmed with tasks; conversely if you produce very general tasks then you may miss out key areas that will need attention. The following examples give some indication of the levels of detail used in different projects.

Example   Tasks: a project to develop a student learning resource on plagiarism

Load questions into learning environment
Produce sample questions
Pilot sample questions

Example   Tasks: a digitization project

Purchase hardware and software

Install new systems

Test new systems

Example   Tasks: relocating a library

Purchase additional shelving

Move books into skips

Re-shelve books

Produce new guiding

In addition to the specific tasks that need to be carried out to complete the project you also need to consider the recurrent tasks, i.e. those that are repeated at regular intervals throughout the project. Examples of recurrent tasks might be regular project team meetings, sending out a weekly project news bulletin and updating the project spreadsheet. These recurrent tasks are sometimes omitted at the project scheduling stage and they can mean that there is a serious underestimate of the amount of time spent on the project.

At this stage in the scheduling process it is also worthwhile thinking about and identifying milestones: significant landmarks in the life of a project. A milestone is *not* a task or an activity but a sign that a stage has been completed in the project. Examples of milestones include project start, project end, end of Phase 1, completion of staff training and completion of installation of new hardware and software. Milestones provide important markers to the project manager and team as they may be used to signal to the stakeholders that the project is on course. Milestones can also be motivators for the project workers as they show them that their work is producing outcomes.

One approach to capturing this information is to write the name of each task on a Post-it™ note. Give each task a number (starting with 1) as this will come in useful at a later stage. Different coloured Post-it™ notes may be used to indicate the main tasks, recurrent tasks and milestones. The author has used this technique in the initial scheduling meetings of ILS projects and found both that colleagues enjoy using it and that very quickly a whole range of tasks are identified.

Estimating the duration

You will need to estimate the duration or how long each task will. If you are completely new to the type of tasks that will be included in your project schedule then ask an experienced colleague (either from your own ILS or another one) for help. The use of e-mail discussion lists is one way in which you can gain help in estimating the amount of time the different activities will take. Once you have worked out the likely duration of each task then record this information, for example on a Post-it™ note (see Figure 3.3).

Task number		Estimated duration
	Name of task	
Earliest start date		Latest start date

Task number = 14		Estimated duration = 1 day
	Install software	
Earliest start date = 12/11/05		Latest start date = 13/11/05

Figure 3.3   Identification of tasks using Post-it™ notes

Important note

At a later stage in the project scheduling process you will need to estimate the number of staff hours or days that someone will have to spend carrying out the task.

It is worth highlighting the difference between these two different time measurements: the *duration* is the amount of time normally measured in days, weeks or months that a task will take; the *staff time* or *effort* is the amount of time individuals will spend working on that task e.g. two people for eight hours each, four people for four hours each.

Working out the logical sequence of events

The next step is to work out the order of tasks and this involves showing the relationships or dependencies between the different tasks using the logic:

- Finish-to-start, i.e. Task B can start when Task A is complete
- Start-to-start, i.e. Task B can start at the same time as Task C
- Finish-to-finish, i.e. Task C must finish when Task B finishes
- Start-to-finish, i.e. when task B starts Task C must finish.

The Finish-to-start relationship is the most common one that project managers need to deal with and it is illustrated in Figure 3.4, where B can't take place until A is completed.

Figure 3.4   Finish-to-start relationship

If you are developing the project plan using Post-it™ notes then the logic can be added by laying out all the Post-it™ notes on a large piece of paper and drawing in arrows to show the relationships between the tasks. If you are using project management software this result is achieved by linking tasks using task numbers. Whichever method you use the end result is a logic diagram.

You will need to include milestones, of which project schedules will have at least two – start and end. Some tasks will take place sequentially, as in Figure 3.5.

Figure 3.5   Sequential tasks

While other tasks will take place concurrently, as in Figure 3.6.

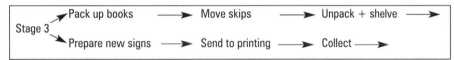

Figure 3.6   Concurrent tasks

Working out the timescale of the project

The critical path is the path through the project that links the critical tasks, i.e. those tasks which if they are not completed on time will result in the project not meeting its deadline. The critical path is illustrated in Figure 3.7 where tasks A, B, C and E each take five days to complete. Task D takes one day to complete. The whole project from task A to task E takes 20 days to complete. If the time taken to complete tasks A, B, C or E slips then the whole project timetable will slip and the project will take longer than expected. In other words tasks A, B, C and E are critical as shown by their shading and the pathway that connects them is the critical path. In contrast if Task D takes between 1 and 10 days to complete then the project will still be on time (as it will take 10 days to complete Tasks B and C).

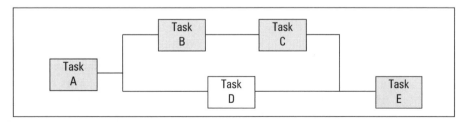

Figure 3.7   Critical path

One method of working out the critical path is to identify the start and end dates for the project. The next step is to work through the tasks starting from the beginning and identifying the earliest start date and earliest finish date for each task. Write these dates on the relevant Post-it™ note (see Figure 3.3). Then work through the tasks starting from the latest finish date identifying the latest start date and latest finish date for each task. Again, write this on the relevant Post-it™ note. The critical path is the set of activities where the earliest and latest finish dates are the same. In other words, their timing is crucial if the project is to remain on schedule. Any time slippages across the critical path have a major impact on the project.

If you create your project plan using project management software then the critical path is automatically worked out for you, is often displayed in red on the screen. This is useful information, as once you know which tasks form the critical path you will know where to put in additional effort if the project deadlines begin to slip.

Presenting your schedule

You will need to present your detailed plan for discussion and approval to the project team, management group and (possibly) the steering committee. There are three main methods of presenting the project plan and these are:

- action plans
- GANTT charts
- PERT diagrams.

Action plans

In simple projects the whole project plan can be illustrated with an action plan that shows who does what and the timescale (see Figure 3.8).

Task	Responsibility	Start date	End date
Book conference facilities	Jane	6 January	15 January
Book speakers	Chris	16 January	31 January
Produce publicity materials	Sam	1 February	28 February
Send out mail shot	Sam	1 March	31 March

Figure 3.8 Action plan

GANTT charts

This shows the tasks that take place within a particular time period, for example a week or month. The technical name for the charts comes from their developer Henry Gantt (1861–1919). They are sometimes also known as bar charts. If you are working on a small project or don't have access to project manager software then you can produce the bar or GANTT charts using a whiteboard and pens, a wall calendar and sticky paper, or a spreadsheet. If you do have access to project manager software (covered in detail in Chapter 7) then it will readily produce a GANTT chart; alternatively you could produce one using a spreadsheet package. Figure 3.9 provides a sample GANTT chart produced on a spreadsheet.

Many project managers use GANTT or bar charts because they are easy to read and can be read by anyone. They clearly show the relationship between the project tasks and the timescale of the project. They will also show recurrent tasks and milestones. It is very easy to look at a GANTT chart and identify times when there may be a pressure on the project, for example as a result of information workers' holidays or peaks in customer demands. However, their disadvantages include the facts that they don't show the relationships between different tasks and they don't show the critical path.

	January	February	March	April
Book conference facilities				
Book speakers				
Produce publicity materials				
Send out mail shot				

Figure 3.9 GANTT chart

PERT diagrams

Another way of obtaining a clear picture and also detailed information about the project is to produce a PERT diagram. PERT stands for Programme Evaluation and Review Technique and this type of diagram was developed in the USA. A PERT diagram shows the logical relationship between the tasks. This may be prepared using a large piece of paper and pen, a whiteboard or project management software. PERT diagrams are very similar to flowcharts and they provide an overview or the 'big picture' of the project. Their advantage over GANTT or bar charts is that they show the relationships between the tasks. PERT diagrams that are produced electronically often have the critical path highlighted in red and this makes it very easy for the project manager to identify those tasks which must be completed on time if the whole project is meet its deadline. However PERT diagrams can be large and difficult to work from. If you use project management software then it can be very difficult to see the whole view of the project on a single screen. A sample PERT diagram is shown in Figure 3.10.

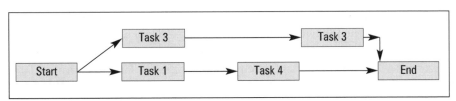

Figure 3.10 PERT diagram

The example presented in Figures 3.8–3.10 is a simple one and it is used to illustrate the main differences between the presentation techniques. Informal research among ILS practitioners suggest that action plans and GANTT charts are the main methods used for planning and presenting project plans. PERT diagrams are commonly used in complex projects where the project manager and team need to work out the logic of a series of related tasks.

Staffing the project

When you are scheduling an activity or project then you need to think about the people side of the work and how you will be able to staff the project:

- Who will be carrying out the work?
- What specialist knowledge or skills do they require?
- How much time will it take them to carry out their project work?

You need to think about how much time each person will have to spend on the project. Are they going to have enough time to complete their project work and also how will this fit into their everyday work?

When you allocate tasks within a team the work may be shared out on the basis of personal interests, job role, experience or expertise, available time or personal development needs. Individuals may volunteer for particular tasks or activities, or they may be asked if they would like to take responsibility for particular tasks. It is important to identify constructive solutions when there are difficulties in agreeing responsibilities. If the team cannot agree responsibilities then it may be worthwhile: identifying preferences; conflicts of preference and constructive solutions.

If library and information workers are assigned to a project it is often on a temporary basis and the project work may be running alongside their main job role. Carroll (2000) advises that if project workers are spending less than 50% of their time on their project work they may have difficulty in prioritizing the project work over their other work. In reality many ILS workers spend less than 50% of their time on project work and this means that they need to be effective time managers if they are to complete their project work. This issue is considered in more depth in Chapter 10.

It is useful to estimate the amount of staff time that is required for a project. You can identify the staff time required for the complex project using a simple equation (found in the majority of standard project management books). To estimate the time a task will take you need to estimate the most pessimistic time (the longest), the average and the most optimistic (the shortest).

The following equation will then help you to work out the most likely time.

$$\text{Time (likely)} = \frac{\text{Time (pessimistic)} + 4 \times \text{Time (average)} + \text{Time (optimistic)}}{6}$$

Example   Estimating staff time

A project team member is estimating the time it will take one person to prepare a mail shot of 500 letters. He estimates the following times:

Most pessimistic time – 12 hours
Average time – 5 hours
Most optimistic time – 3 hours.

What is the likely time this activity will take?
The answer is: approx 5.8 hours
Time (likely) = {12 + (4x5) + 3} ÷ 6

One of the practical dangers of using this type of equation is that it can give the impression of accuracy. In fact the estimate is only as good as the assessment of the optimistic, pessimistic and average times used in the equation. In practice, project managers and teams can improve the accuracy of this process by:

- asking a range of staff for an input into the estimates
- measuring the amount of time it actually takes someone to complete the task
- contacting professional colleagues who have been involved in similar tasks and asking them for their estimates.

In addition to estimating the amount of time that is required to complete particular tasks you also need to consider how many days per month (or year) that someone is able to work on the project. The basic calculation involves identifying the number of days per year and subtracting days for training, weekends, annual leave, statutory days and sick days as follows:

Working = Days in year – (annual leave + weekends + training + statutory
days per   days + sick days)
year
$$= 365 – (20 + 104 + 4 + 11 + 10) = 216 \text{ days per annum}$$

So as a rough rule of thumb someone who is working on a project full time will be available for approximately 216 days' work per year and someone who is spending 50% of their work time on the project will be available for 108 days per year. It is really important to allocate people on the basis of their actual working days per year otherwise you will seriously underestimate the staffing input required for the project.

How will the tasks be carried out?

In the previous sections the project schedule is described in terms of identifying the what, who and when of the project. An important aspect of project management is thinking about *how* the work will be carried out. This is likely to result in the production of a detailed set of procedures plus guidance on the required standards of work. The detailed procedures will then be followed by all the staff working on that part of the project. Detailed procedures or protocols are produced in a wide range of projects e.g. digitization projects, the development of information systems, the movement of library collections. They are particularly important for complex projects involving different teams of information workers who are widely distributed geographically. McDonald (1994) provides a brief and extremely useful guide to moving a library and this covers the type of detailed thinking that needs to go into the planning stage to ensure that the right books end up on the correct shelf in the correct sequence! The complexity of this type of situation is illustrated in the following example.

Example   Moving a library

This is an extensive quotation included here to demonstrate the type of clear thinking and detailed planning that are needed if you are involved in a complicated project such as this one at the Dublin City Library where staff were involved in moving a library and also reorganizing its collection at the same time.

'STOCK MEASUREMENT PROCESS

Central to the success of the move was the development of a reliable stock measurement system. A weeding project was completed prior to measurement. To measure the stock, library attendants carried out a count of the number of shelves and the number of bays in the old library. It was not considered necessary to count the actual items on the shelves. The library collection had expanded greatly over the years and many journals, indexes and abstracts etc. were housed in various storerooms throughout the old library building. It was intended to integrate these items into the new library 's main collection, therefore, the stock held in storerooms had to be included in the stock measurement information.

NEW LIBRARY LAYOUT

The new library's layout has a Reception Desk, Information Points, Reference and Short Loan collections on the ground floor. The Archives/storerooms are on the lower ground floor. The first and second floors are designated subject floors housing both main lending books and journals relating to a particular subject. Thus, the ground floor houses general reference material and short loan collection, the first floor – Business, Humanities and Education, and the second floor – Science, Engineering and Nursing. This represents a radical departure from our traditional arrangement, with material arranged by type rather than subject. This of course added an extra complexity to the move. The collection was not being transferred as a whole to the new location, rather it was being transferred and totally re-organised.

SHELF SPACE

To calculate shelf space, a unit of shelving, back and front was referred to as a bay and contained between 5–7 rows of shelves on each side. The height of the bay was determined by the collection to be housed. Bays of shelving for journals were to be at a lower height than books. With accurate stock information, including approximate expansion estimates for each collection and knowledge of the new library's layout and shelf space, the amount of shelf space to be assigned for each Dewey sequence range was then calculated.

GROUND FLOOR

The organisation of the ground floor was the least complicated. However, as the Reference area was located close to the Reception Desk, the visual impact of the displayed collections was important. Consequently, some collections were re-arranged to ensure that 'elegant ' bound volumes were visible when entering the new library building!

FIRST AND SECOND SUBJECT FLOORS

The planning and organisation of the two subject floors was more extensive. Working from enlarged photocopies of the new building and our stock measurement figures, each collection was highlighted by using a different colour. Shelving space was then allocated.

DEVISING A TRANSFER CODING SYSTEM

A Transfer Coding System was required to ensure that each book in the old library, including those in storerooms, arrived at the correct destination in the new library. The system of coding decided upon was a colour–number–letter sequence. Each floor of the new building was assigned a colour, white for the lower ground floor, blue for the ground floor, red for the first floor and yellow for the second floor. As shelf dimensions in the two libraries were identical, a shelf for shelf transfer was possible. Each unit (a unit being one side of a bay of 5–7 shelves) was assigned an individual number to denote the unit, and each shelf in the unit was assigned a letter. For example, shelves were marked 1A,1B . . . 1F. The next bay would be 2A . . . 2F, etc. This system ensured that each shelf would be uniquely marked with the colour of the floor, the name of the collection and the sequence.

LABELLING SHELVES

To commence the process of labelling, a colour coded A4 card, indicating the shelf number, collection details and subject floor was attached to shelves. These cards were written in duplicate (for the old and the new library). A wider group of staff was involved when the labelling of each individual shelf commenced. Coloured, easy-peel, self-adhesive labels, supplied by the moving company, were also used. (These labels were later removed by the moving company and attached to crates). An inventory of all shelf numbers was maintained. Based on this inventory, labels were hand-written using the colour–number–letter sequence originally devised on the transfer coding system.

MARKING PLANS

To correctly shelve material in the new library, shelving plans of the new library as well as shelves in the new library had to be marked using the same coding system i.e. colour–number–sequence. When marking the shelving plans, 1–3 shelves were left free on each unit of shelving to facilitate the estimates of expansion. An inventory of stock in the storerooms was also factored into the plans and this determined what shelf numbers were assigned to each unit of shelving. This was one of the most complicated tasks and required staff to work in small teams moving from shelf to shelf in the old library marking the shelf numbers onto the new plans. It was an arduous process but the five weeks of detailed preparation ensured its smooth execution.

LABELLING SHELVES IN NEW LIBRARY

A coloured A4 card with collection details and shelf number was attached to each shelf in the new library to guarantee the correct destination of material. Once again the team was increased at this stage to complete this task as we were now working to a tight schedule in anticipation of the movers' arrival.

THE MOVING COMPANY

Early in the pre-move phase, tenders were invited from moving companies. The decision to select the moving company was based on the company's previous experience of moving libraries. During discussions with the selected company, it was agreed that the work would be completed over a period of 18 days. It was agreed that if necessary work would be carried out on Saturday and Sundays. The company agreed to supply an agreed number of one-metre crates. Each crate would hold one shelf of books, regardless of the number of books on the shelf. Five hundred crates were to be moved each day. Crates were to be packed, unpacked, transported and re-shelved by the moving company' (Allen and Bowden, 2001, pp.13–15).

Reporting process

At the initial planning stages it is worthwhile starting to think about how the project manager will obtain information about the project's progress. This process will be refined in more detail after the production of the detailed project plan. In general, the project manager needs to obtain information about the progress of the project, for example from team workers, and this information will enable you to identify:

- feedback on progress of project plan
  — significant dates and milestones
  — significant constraints
  — potential problems
  — existing problems
  — creep in project time
  — slack in project time
- feedback from other ILS staff and stakeholders (including customers).

The project manager will also need to report the project progress to their managers and stakeholders. The following groups will need to be kept informed about the project's progress:

- project steering group
- project management team
- funding organization
- ILS staff and customers
- stakeholders
- senior managers.

The type of reports used to keep everyone informed will depend on the project and all the different stakeholders. Common reports include management reports, milestone reports and financial reports. The structure of the reports will vary from informal to extremely formal reports. Externally funded projects generally have very strict rules about reporting and will specify the reporting process, including form and report templates. It is worthwhile spending some time at the start of the project in identifying the reporting requirements as this will mean you can set up the appropriate systems to provide the necessary information for the reports. This means that the reporting process is well managed and doesn't involve last-minute panics as the project manager and team discover they haven't collected the correct information.

At the end of the project the project manager often needs to write formal reports, for example a final report, a final financial report. This process may include an internal project evaluation and review reports. Many projects are also reviewed by an external agency and this results in an external project evaluation and review form. Again, it is worthwhile thinking about the final project reports at the start of the project process as it means you can plan for their production throughout the project process. This topic is covered in Chapter 5.

The following examples show the types of reports that may be required by the sponsors of externally funded projects.

Example   JISC Information Environment Development Programmes

The JISC website provides guidance on the reporting requirements for each project. Each project is required to provide two reports per year and they are informed of the timescale for submitting reports. JISC IE provides templates for reports and these can be seen at their website. See www.jisc.ac.uk.

Example   European-funded reports

Projects that are funded by the Europe Union, for example European Social Fund (ESF)-supported projects require a series of reports to be submitted by the project manager. These reports summarize spending on the project and the achievement of the project outcomes. The ESF enables the project manager to determine the frequency of the reports in some projects, e.g. monthly or quarterly reports. The submission of these reports triggers payment of the project grant. See www.europeansocialfund.gov.uk.

Working out the finances

At this stage, the finances need to be worked out. This is considered in Chapter 6.

Identifying potential problems

The idea of a risk analysis was introduced in Chapter 2 with a simple methodology for carrying one out. As you approach the end of the planning process it is worthwhile re-doing the risk analysis as you will now have a more in-depth understanding of the project and what it entails. The results of the risk analysis will be included in the project plan.

Producing the project plan

The output of the planning stage is a project plan and this will be used as a formal working document by project workers. There are a number of methods of producing this. In very large and complex projects the project plan may be written up in the form of a detailed specification identifying the detail of the project process, the resource requirements and the boundaries of the project. In small and relatively simple projects the project manager and team can produce a simple plan. Both of these types of project plans are outlined below.

Project specification

Large and complex projects, and particularly those involving different units, departments or organizations, do require a project specification. The project specification may be used as a tool for deciding and confirming the boundaries and details of the project, as well as the responsibilities of key staff. It is an important document and once agreed lays down the project parameters. Any changes to the project will require the re-negotiation of the project specification. For the project manager the specification can be a valuable tool, if only because it can be used to prevent stakeholders (including senior manages and directors) from moving the goalposts and changing the project outcomes or resources without discussions and/or the agreement of the project manager and management team. Different organizations have their own standard project specification template but, typically, the specification covers the following topics.

Example Typical structure of a project specification

Introduction
Purpose
Background
Goals and objectives
Scope and limitations
Strategy
Description of main activities
Project schedule
Resources
Finance
List of staff and their involvement
Connections to other activities
Transitional arrangements
Communication strategy
Management structure
Reporting schedule
Risks
Quality standards, processes and procedures
Intellectual property, patents and licences
Insurance
Distribution list
Formal approval (signature, name, date)

In practice the contents of project specifications will vary depending on the project and, in some instances, they may be called by other names such as definition, plan or strategy.

The following example shows the structure of a project specification which was 'designed to facilitate communication between the various parties involved in the

WebLaw project. It aims to set out the objectives, description, methodology, organization, timeline and budget of the project' (WebLaw, 2003).

Example   WebLaw project management plan

Contents
1. Introduction
   - 1.1 Purpose of this project plan
   - 1.2 Project objectives and deliverables
     - 1.2.1 Objectives
     - 1.2.2 Deliverables
   - 1.3 Overview of the project
     - 1.3.1 Project description
     - 1.3.2 Phasing of the project
     - 1.3.3 Activities to be performed
2. Project definition
   - 2.1 Project organization
     - 2.1.1 Project team structure
       - 2.1.1.1 Project implementation committee
       - 2.1.1.2 Project steering committee
       - 2.1.1.3 Project team
       - 2.1.1.4 Reference group
   - 2.2 Project communication
     - 2.2.1 Meetings
     - 2.2.2 Discussion lists
     - 2.2.3 Webpage
   - 2.3 Project constraints
     - 2.3.1 Project risk management
   - 2.4 Project timeline
   - 2.5 Project budget
3. Work plan
   - 3.1 Work plan assumptions
   - 3.2 Work breakdown structure
   - 3.3 External guideline compliance
4. Project reporting
   - 4.1 Informal reporting
   - 4.2 Formal reporting

Simple project plans

In relatively small projects there is no need to produce sophisticated project plans. It is often sufficient to produce a project plan that contains:

- project brief
- action plan
- details of staffing implications
- financial requirements
- risk analysis.

Communicating the project plan

Once you have produced the project plan then you need to communicate it to the relevant people. If the project team worked together to collaboratively to produce the plan they are likely to feel ownership over it. If the project manager has produced the plan him or herself then they will need to 'sell' the plan to the project team, the management team and, if appropriate, the steering committee.

If you have produced a very detailed project specification then, in addition to submitting the full plan to relevant people, you may need to break it down and present different parts of the plan to different audiences as indicated in the following example.

Example   Communicating the plan

The author was involved in a project concerned with closing a university learning resource centre and moving its contents to three locations. This project involved working with the university's estate staff. At her first meeting with the estate operations manager she handed him a copy of the project plan (88 pages of A4). He was horrified. She quickly realized that her detailed plan had resulted in information overload and agreed to send him a one-page overview and then weekly summaries of what needed to be moved where each week. It was a salutary lesson in communication skills!

In many projects the approval to go ahead is made on the basis of the project plan. This makes the project plan a crucial document. Once you have gained approval for your project then you can move on to the next stage: project implementation.

Summary

This chapter considers the 'nuts and bolts' of project planning: researching the project, detailed planning and finally documenting and communicating the plan. Research needs to be carried out both within the ILS and also in the wider professional context so that the project manager and team are able to learn from good practice and have a good grasp of the context of the project. The project planning process involves producing a project plan that outlines the tasks that need to be carried out, timescale and the resource requirements (in terms of people and finance). In large complex projects the planning process may result in a detailed project specification while in smaller projects the project plan may be contained in a short report.

References

Allen, J. and Bowden, L. (2001) Move Over: moving DCU library's print material to the new library building, *SCONUL Newsletter*, **24**, (Winter), 13–16, www.sconul.ac.uk.

Carroll, J. (2000) *Project 2000 in Easysteps*, Southam, Computer Step.

Hall, F. (2002) How to Install an Access Control System in less than 4 Months and Live to Tell the Tale, *SCONUL Newsletter*, **25**, (Spring), 87–9, www.sconul.ac.uk.

McDonald, A. (1994) *Moving Your Library*, London, Aslib/IMI.

Thompson, C (2003) The implementation of an Automated Telephone Renewals Service at Northumbria University Library, *SCONUL Newsletter*, **28**, (Spring), 25–7, www.sconul.ac.uk/.

WebLaw (2003) *Project Documents*, http://weblaw.edu.au/weblaw.

4

Implementation

Introduction

Once the project has been planned and the project manager has received permission to go ahead then the implementation process starts and the project manager and team will work on the project until it is complete. This chapter explores the implementation and project completion process, and it provides guidance on what to do if things go wrong.

Implementing the project

This stage involves putting the plan into action and actually 'doing' the project. The implementation phase involves managing the following:

- people
- resources
- project process.

The people side of project management is covered in more detail in Chapter 10 and the financial side is covered in Chapter 6. In this section we will focus on the project process which involves monitoring, tracking and, where necessary, taking corrective action. Effective project managers are people who are able to juggle many different tasks and issues, and respond proactively to problems and challenges as they arise during the project implementation process.

Although you will have a detailed project plan, it is unlikely that everything will go exactly to plan. Your risk analysis will have identified potential trouble spots and these all need careful monitoring. In real-life projects a diverse range of factors can intervene with adverse effects. Some examples include:

- staff sickness
- late arrival of equipment
- technical failures of equipment or software
- inaccurate estimations of the amount of time it will take to complete a task
- changes in the price of essential supplies
- failure to get permission to go ahead with a particular aspect of the project
- change in requirements by funding organization or sponsor
- unexpected events, e.g. fire, flood, landslide.

Monitoring the tasks

As project manager you need to monitor tasks, blockages and slippage, match of plan with reality, expenditure, quality, complex changes to the plan. Reiss (1995) identifies two approaches to monitoring progress:

- DIY – Do-It-Yourself, i.e. wander around and talk with people, observe what is happening and ask for printouts as and when you think it is appropriate. One of the advantages of this approach is that sometimes small problems or potential problems can be identified extremely early in the project process and a solution can be worked out with the team involved in that part of the project.
- OPE – Other People's Effort, i.e. you ask other people to measure progress and report back to you at regular intervals. In large and complex projects there is normally a formal reporting process as described in Chapter 3. Problems and potential problems may then be identified and addressed through regular meetings or, if they are relatively small, by e-mail or phone conversations.

The majority of project managers use a mixture of these two methods depending on their context and the nature of the project.

At the same time it is useful to measure the accuracy of estimates of staff time. In projects involving different people who are perhaps working on different sites then a simple process such as everyone e-mailing the project manager with information about the state of all the tasks at set times each week will give the manager the necessary information. The pro-forma in Figure 4.1 may be used.

Weekly progress report from _____

Task number & date	Start date	End date	Current status/comments

Major concerns/issues:

Signature:

Date:

Figure 4.1   Sample weekly progress report

The following is an example of how progress may be tracked across a disparate team.

Example   Monitoring tasks in a library move

This project involved the movement, merging and integration of five libraries in one UK government department. As a means of keeping track of the tasks allocated to each project team member, the project administrator e-mailed each team member once a week and asked them to report back on the status of their weekly tasks. Anyone who didn't reply to this e-mail within 24 hours received a follow-up phone call. Although the administrator gained the nickname 'Miss Whiplash' as a result of this activity she was able to ensure that all tasks were closely monitored and the project achieved its outcomes.

The larger and the more complex the project then the more challenging it is to keep track of all the tasks. As project manager it is important that you keep track of the tasks and particularly those tasks that are on the critical path. Project management software such as MS Project (see Chapter 7) is very useful in helping to manage the information relating to the ongoing status of tasks and it will provide reports such as GANTT charts, completed tasks or part-completed tasks, tasks that have not yet been started or work remaining on part-completed tasks, daily or weekly task lists and individual task lists.

If you are managing a complex project and set up systems to keep you informed of the status of individual tasks it is also worthwhile actually checking up that the work has occurred. This is particularly true if you are working with people you don't know very well, e.g. contractors. This is illustrated in the following example.

Example   Installation of new computers

The author was involved in the reorganization of a college learning support centre where one of the tasks was the unpacking and installing of 50 new computers. In a regular weekly phone conversation the Director of Computing Systems informed me that the new computers had arrived and been installed in the IT room. As I ticked the task off on my project action plan I thought I'd just check up on it. Walking into the IT room I found the computers were there but hadn't been installed. The temporary technician had misinformed the Director! Fortunately there was still sufficient time to install the computers before the arrival of the students. This example taught me an important lesson – check that the work has been carried out.

It is at the implementation stage that the critical path analysis becomes very important. As discussed in Chapter 3, the critical path is the series of tasks that if delayed will mean that the project will not be completed on time. As project manager it is vital that you monitor the tasks on the critical path: it is here that remedial action needs to be swiftly introduced if the project is to be delivered on time. The easiest way to do this is to ask people to stop working on the non-critical tasks (in terms of the timescale of the project) and move to the critical tasks.

Identifying problems and potential problems

In many respects the project implementation process is about identifying problems or potential problems and then developing strategies or interventions for dealing with them. Reiss (1995) provides a useful metaphor for problem solving:

> A project manager is rather like someone standing on the top of a cliff watching a ship come into harbour. The ship is a problem and the harbour is the project manager and team's time and attention. At first the ship is on the horizon and looks small and insignificant. As the ship comes closer it demands attention and may cause the project manager not to see other ships that are now arriving on the horizon. By dealing with the ship that is coming into harbour other problems or ships are gathering on the horizon and will soon move forward into the harbour. The moral is to deal with problems while they are still on the horizon rather than when they arrive in the centre of the project demanding lots of time and attention.

During the implementation stage of a project the manager and team need to be on the lookout for problems or potential problems. The following are the most common kinds:

- blockages
- project slippage
- quality issues
- complex issues.

These are dealt with in turn below.

Blockages

The project manager's role involves identifying and responding to these events so that they don't undermine the successful completion of the project. Here is a list of some of the situations that could arise within a project:

- staff sickness
- staff move to another position
- inaccuracy of estimates of time to carry out work
- unexpected technical difficulties
- failure of contractors to fulfil their commitment

- unexpected delays on building work or installation of systems
- legal problems, e.g. with respect to copyright
- unexpected health and safety issues.

Strategies for dealing with blockages include building in time for problems into the original project plan and/or including a contingency fund. Many project managers build in 20% time for unexpected blockages and, if this time is not required, then they will complete the project early. A contingency fund of up to 20% is sometimes built into projects but many externally funded ones don't allow for this type of practice although money can be vired from one budget heading to another (see Chapter 6). The following examples show some of the kinds of blockages that may arise during a project.

Example An infestation of fleas

Despite the most well thought-out and detailed project plans, the reality of implementing a project often throws up unexpected events or situations. For example, the author was once involved in moving an existing library into a new building. Movement of shelving and stock provided the right environment for the hatching of previously dormant fleas' eggs, and the resulting infestation of fleas caused the library to be closed for a number of days while the environmental health people tackled the problem. Fortunately our contingency planning had resulted in us building in two weeks' slack in the project timetable and although the fleas cost us one of these weeks it didn't adversely affect the project outcomes.

Example Moving a library

The example of moving the Dublin City Library was first introduced in Chapter 3 and it is included here too as it illustrates some of the challenges that will be thrown at project managers. This example is concerned with delays in transporting stock and also delays in accessing lifts.

'The major consideration was to keep a steady flow of crates moving between libraries. A system was devised whereby one team would pack the crates and transport them to the new library. When removed from the vans, they would be brought to the relevant floors for shelving. It was envisaged that the empty vans would then return to the old library and the process would recommence. Unfortunately, delays in the schedule commenced almost immediately as it took longer than anticipated to move the containers to the transit vans. It was decided to close one floor to users, and an efficient exit point was re-routed though this area. Notices were displayed advising users of the closure; however, as this was the quietest time of the year, there was minimum disruption. The solution agreed was to have the movers load the crates and wheel them to the exit point, then slide them down the stairs to the waiting transit vans!

A further delay occurred when the movers could not gain easy access to the lifts in the new library because of demand by other deliveries of furnishings, equipment, fittings etc. This resulted in crates piling up, not only in transit vans, but also in both libraries. A solution was eventually found when priority was given to the moving company over any other deliveries. This saw an end to any further difficulties.' (Allen and Bowden, 2001, p.15)

Example   A flood in a toilet

The author was involved in an e-learning project that provided staff development for staff in a range of universities across the world. It involved a series of 21-day online workshops, each run with extremely tight deadlines. The project team was made up of staff from three UK universities. On Day 5 of the second workshop a toilet overflowed downstairs and, as a result, brought down the server which supported the project. This was potentially disastrous and project participants were quickly e-mailed (by a member of staff in a different university) to explain what had happened and also to assure them that the project would be up and running again as soon as possible. The technical team had diligently backed up the project records each night and also had access to another server. They worked hard and managed to get the whole project up and running again within hours. Only a relatively small amount of data was lost. The whole project quickly got on track again.

In practice, during the implementation of a project the project manager's time is likely to be spent troubleshooting and problem solving. Project team meetings and management meetings are the place to discuss and, hopefully, resolve blockages.

Project slippage

Slippage occurs when it takes longer than anticipated to complete particular tasks and so it becomes impossible to adhere to the project schedule. Once the project manager has identified that the schedule is slipping and different tasks may not be completed on time then there are a number of different common responses:

- *Obtain additional resources*, e.g. obtain more people to work on the project. While this may appear to be an attractive option, common experience in IT projects suggests that simply adding more staff to the project may delay the project even further! The new people will need time to be trained and work up to speed with the project and so may take time away from the current project team. Carefully introducing a small number of additional people does sometimes produce benefits; this is often when they are given very specific tasks to complete and ones with which they are very familiar.

- *Ask people to work harder or to work longer hours.* In the short term this strategy can work. If there is money available in the budget then paying some additional overtime can pay dividends. However if this is used as a long-term solution it can de-motivate staff and lead to stress, burn-out and an increase in sick leave or staff turnover.
- *Reviewing the project and reducing its scope.* Sometimes slippage can be dealt with by reviewing the scope of the project and either cutting out some of the project outcomes or postponing them until after the project has been officially 'completed'.
- *Accepting the slippage and renegotiating a new end date.* Sometimes this is the most sensible course of action as the implementation process often reveals blockages or problems that hadn't been anticipated at the planning stage.

Quality issues

The quality of the work needs to be monitored to ensure that you meet the required standards. The detailed project plan is likely to include information about the quality criteria and also how these will be checked. Individuals responsible for monitoring quality need to be proactive and start off their quality processes and procedures from the beginning of the project. They also need to report their findings to the project team and manager on a regular basis. This will enable appropriate adjustments to be made to the working practices of the project team extremely quickly.

Complex issues

In complex projects a relatively small change in one part of the system may result in unexpected and unwelcome changes in other parts of the system. This is the often-mentioned 'chaos theory' where the apparent beating of a butterfly wing in one part of the world may result in unexpected and unwelcome weather conditions in another continent. One of the challenges of managing this type of situation is that they are unexpected and sometimes by attempting to put right the problem the project manager and team may introduce even greater problems, leading to an unravelling of the entire project plan. In this type of situation it is often best to let the system find a new steady-state before attempting to impose order on it. This is illustrated in the following example.

Example   The potential unravelling of an information literacy programme.

A new module called 'Academic and professional practice' was introduced into the undergraduate curriculum of a UK university business school. The aim of this module was to teach 450 new undergraduates the following skills:

- study skills
- information searching
- ICT skills
- team work skills
- quantitative methods.

The module was delivered by a team made up of eight lecturers, four ICT trainers and two academic librarians. Each week students had to attend a general lecture and an ICT lecture and workshop and, in addition to their weekly sessions, every four weeks they also attended an information skills workshop and a small group tutorial session. The timetable was complex as students were allocated to their individual sessions on the basis of their degree programme.

In Week 2 severe timetabling clashes took place with the ICT lectures and workshops. The 'butterfly' in this instance was a change in a timetable within another faculty which had an impact on 5% of the business school students. As a result the whole timetable began to fall apart. The initial response of the module team was to reorganize the ICT lectures and workshops and reallocate all the students to new sessions. This would have taken at least two full days to organize and everyone was already working at full capacity.

However, the team decided to change their approach and instead of allocating students to lectures and workshops they explained the situation to the students and asked them to sign up for the sessions that most suited their needs. Over the next four days the students could be seen clustered around notice boards with their timetables. Many of the sign-up sheets became dog-eared as students signed up and then changed their minds about the sessions. Finally, the 450 students had organized themselves into new groups and reported to the teaching team that they much preferred this arrangement as it meant they could fit their ICT sessions around their other activities. The staff were pleased too – the solution was effective and the students were satisfied. The teaching team decided to use this approach to organizing lectures and workshops in future years.

Communicating and reporting

During the implementation process the project manager and team need to carry out their internal and external communication strategies. This involves implementing and monitoring communication processes within the project management team and also communicating news and information about the project to a wider audience. This topic is considered in more detail in Chapter 5.

At this stage in the project, the manager will be focused on three different aspects of the project: individuals, project teams and the actual project process. The project manager will be receiving information from a number of different sources such as:

- individual team members
- team meetings
- management meetings
- computerized information systems
- observation of work activities.

One of the important activities that the project manager is likely to be involved in is collating this information, using the information to update and/or change the project plan, and presenting this information to the project team, management team and/or steering group and/or funding body or sponsor in the form of a progress report. Figures 4.2 and 4.3 provide outline structures for such reports.

Sample: Project progress report

Project title:
Report written by: Date of report:
Report covers period:

1. Key achievements in the last three months:

2. Performance against project plan
     a. Has there been any variance from the agreed project plan?
        If 'yes' please indicate what the variance is and who it has been agreed with:
     b. Will the project plan need to be revised?
        If 'yes' please state what revisions are required and why:

3. Please outline any problems impeding progress and action being taken:

4. Please outline any unresolved problems from the last report:

5. Please identify any unexpected outcomes or benefits from the project:

6. Please outline lessons learnt during this period:

7. Any additional notes/comments:

Figure 4.2   Sample progress report
Based on an example obtained from University of Birmingham, Information Services, Learning Development Unit, Project Progress Report (www.weblearn.bham.ac.uk/new/bham/ldu_examples.htm)

Title
1.   Background
2.   Project aims and objectives
3.   Summary of achievements over XXX time period
4.   Update on work packages
      4.1 Project management (work package 1)
      4.2 Pilot and demonstrator product (work packages 2, 3 & 4)
      4.3 Sustainability (work package 5)
      4.4 Promotional materials (work package 4)
      4.5 Dissemination (work package 6)
5.   References
6.   Appendices
      A: Work packages and timetables.

Figure 4.3   Sample progress report
This example comes from: Beard, J. and de Vekey (2003)

Reviewing the project process

Throughout the project implementation stage there is a need for the project manager and team to review the project process. This enables problems and potential problems to be identified and, hopefully, corrected. Many teams include a project review as part of the agenda of their regular meetings. Structures and approaches to reviewing the project are outlined in Chapters 5 and 8.

Project completion

Once the project is approaching completion the project manager and team need to focus on managing the following processes and activities:

- project outcomes
- project reports
- loose ends
- hand-over
- celebration.

The project manager and team need to check that all the project outcomes have been achieved. It is likely that there have been unexpected project outcomes too and it is worthwhile identifying these and recording them. Examples of unexpected project outcomes could include additional publicity for the ILS, increased confidence in staff or development of a 'live' network of like-minded people. Keeping track of the achievement of project outcomes is important: these may be used to convince potential funders or sponsors in the future that the ILS is able to deliver the goods.

The project completion stage normally involves writing up the project reports; in large and complex projects, sometimes six months will be set aside for this task at the end of the project. Typically project reports will include management reports, finance reports and reports to sponsors. These reports are all vital as they ensure that all the relevant people (including the information and library profession as a whole) get to hear about and learn from the project. The topic of project reports is covered in some detail in Chapter 5.

It is also important to identify and tie up any loose ends. This is particularly important in projects involving contract staff who are likely to leave at the end of the project. Who will deal with late-arriving invoices or queries about the project? Who will provide references for the departing project team? How will the stakeholders be informed of the completion of the project? Spending some time identifying and developing processes for managing loose ends is important. Otherwise the host organization or staff who have not been actively involved in the project will inherit time-consuming and messy work and this can cause conflict.

With many information and library projects, e.g. the implementation of a new IT system, moving a library into a new building, there is a hand-over stage when the project ceases to be a project and becomes part of the normal operations. In these types of projects it is important that there is a clear hand-over process so that the day-to-day operations manager and their team are clearly briefed about managing the new system or building and realize that it is now their responsibility. At the same time the project manager needs to 'let go' of the project and move on to other duties.

One common problem identified by participants on project management courses is the difficulty in completing and closing projects. These practitioners said that in their ILS (predominately UK academic and government-based services) they found it difficult to actually close projects and, as a result, some projects appeared to creep on over time, devouring resources and de-motivating staff. Effective strategies for dealing with this situation were identified as:

- identifying clear project aims, outcomes, action plan and end date
- raising the issue at staff meetings and ensuring that staff were instructed to stop work on all project work
- handing over all remaining project work to an individual or small operations team and giving them responsibility for tying up loose ends
- formally closing the project.

Finally, a good way to end any project is to celebrate the project's successes and the scale of this celebration will vary from tea and cakes through to a large-scale party.

Example   Moving a library

Allen and Bowden (2001, p.16) describe the project management of the move of 250,000 items into a new library and describe the satisfaction of the project completion as follows:

'As originally planned the new state of the art library opened its doors, fully operational, to its first student on the first day of the new semester in September 2000. The opening went so smoothly that few would have guessed the logistics involved in getting this dispersed collection of books to the relevant subject floors. Did we meet the challenge? The ultimate success of the method of moving used was very apparent, given that all library material was in the correct place by the correct time. Essentially, no more than a handful of books were out of place – or even upside down! Was it straightforward? Yes and no. Yes – in that the books were assigned a unique place in the new library and no – in that this required meticulous planning and a great deal of hard work. Apart from the hard work involved in this complex operation, there is little doubt that the success of such a move could not have been achieved without the support, encouragement and above all, the good humour of DCU library staff.'

Summary

This chapter is concerned with implementing the project, which involves the project manager in managing individuals, the team and the project process. A wide range of strategies exist for managing problems in the project process such as slippage, blockages or complex problems. In all of these situations it is important that the project manager and team reflect on the situation before intervening; otherwise there is the danger that their intervention will make matters worse. Finally the chapter outlines the steps that need to be taken to close a project and hand it over.

References

Allen, J. and Bowden, L. (2001) Move Over: moving DCU library's print material to the new library building, *SCONUL Newsletter*, **24**, (Winter), 13–16, www.sconul.ac.uk.

Beard, J. and de Vekey, J. (2003) *Progress Report: British Library Co-operation and Partnership Programme No. 6: working with public libraries to enhance access to quality-assured health information for the lay public*, **2**, (12 February), 1–4.

Reiss (1995) *Project Management Demystified: today's tools and techniques*, 2nd edn, London, Spon Press.

5

Evaluation and dissemination

Introduction

This chapter is concerned with project evaluation and methods of disseminating the outcomes of the project. A formal project evaluation process is often required by the funders or sponsors of projects and, in all types of projects, they are an important means of learning from the experience. Individuals working on small, local projects may feel pressurized to move on to the next project as soon as their current one is complete but if they fail to reflect on and evaluate their work then there is the danger that mistakes will be repeated and lessons not learned. It is common practice to disseminate the outcomes of a project both as a means for gaining publicity for the project and ILS and also to help share good practice and lessons learnt within the library and information profession. Dissemination of the outcomes of the evaluation process is considered in the second part of this chapter, which covers reports, conference papers and presentations, and websites.

Project evaluation

An important part of the project completion process is the project evaluation, which is carried out for a number of different reasons. As a management tool it enables the project manager and others to identify their effectiveness, areas of strength and weakness, and lessons for the future. The outcomes of the evaluation process such as reports may be used to disseminate good practice and lessons learnt within the information and library community. In this way they can act as a marketing tool and also as a means of career progress for individuals. The funders or sponsors of projects will normally require some kind of evaluation process to be carried out. Finally a user group or other agency may become involved in evaluating the project.

The project evaluation process involves finding answers to questions such as:

- Did the project achieve its outcomes?
- Did the project achieve any unexpected outcomes?
- Did the project manage to be on time and within budget, and to produce work to the required quality?
- What was the impact of the project on customers, colleagues and other stakeholders?
- What was the impact of the project on other library systems and services?

- What did we learn from the project?
- What will we do differently next time we run a project?

The results of the evaluation will provide evidence of the impact of the project on services, products and people, and this may be used in the future to obtain additional funding or support for new projects.

It is worthwhile considering who will carry out the evaluation process. In relatively small and local projects the evaluation may be carried out by the project manager or one of his or her colleagues. The obvious disadvantage of asking the project manager to evaluate the project is that they are likely to be biased (either intentionally or unconsciously) and stakeholders may find it difficult to provide them with honest feedback if they know that person well. In many large and complex projects the evaluation process may be carried out by a member of staff with special responsibility for research or quality issues or by an external evaluator or a consultant.

If the project is externally funded then the funding body or sponsor may require an evaluation. This may be carried out by the funder themselves or someone who is contracted by them or it may be carried out by the project team for the funder. The funders may be motivated by different reasons, for example to justify their expenditure to their sponsors, to demonstrate the success of the project and its outcomes and/or to identify areas for improvement (both for themselves as funders and also the project organization). The advantages and disadvantages of different people leading the evalution process are summarized in Table 5.1.

Table 5.1 Leading the evaluation process

	Advantages	Disadvantages
Project manager or someone closely involved in project process	Knows the project and its processes. Knows the stakeholders. Carries out the evaluation as part of their project work.	May be biased. May not have very good evaluation skills.
Colleague from same organization	Understands the context. Carries out the evaluation as part of their 'normal' work and doesn't require additional payment. Enables them to learn more about the project.	May be biased. May not have very good evaluation skills.
Colleague from same organization with specialist role, e.g. researcher, evaluator, quality control	Understands the context. Has very good evaluation skills. Carries out the evaluation as part of their 'normal' work and doesn't require additional payment. Enables them to learn more about the project.	May be biased.

Continued on next page

Table 5.1 *Continued*

	Advantages	Disadvantages
Consultant or external researcher	Has very good evaluation skills. Unbiased. Takes additional time to get to understand the project and its context. Ideally has experience of evaluating a wide range of projects and can bring with them a broader perspective.	Takes time to identify appropriate person and ensure that they have the relevant skills. May be relatively expensive as needs to be paid in 'real' money. May not understand specific context.
Funding organization or their representative	May have very good evaluation skills. Will bring in an external perspective and experience of evaluating a wide range of projects.	May not have very good evaluation skills. May focus on a fixed or limited set of evaluation criteria. May not understand the context or specific project.

Different projects will base their project evaluation process around different parameters. This section will focus on two different approaches: a simple method relevant for small-scale projects involving relatively small numbers of people, and a comprehensive method that may be used within large-scale and complex projects.

In relatively small-scale projects a simple evaluation process is normally sufficient. One technique that the author has used is to ask appropriate people, for example project team members and other stakeholders, four questions:

- What did the project achieve?
- What went well during the project?
- What did you learn from the project?
- What would you do differently if you were to repeat the project?

A simple way of obtaining this information is to divide a piece of flipchart paper, a whiteboard or even a sheet of A4 paper into four and designate a space for each of the questions. Individuals or small groups can then complete the questions and their answers can be included in the final project reports. This is illustrated in Figure 5.1.

What did the project achieve?	What went well during the project?
What did you learn from the project?	What would you do differently if you were to repeat the project?

Figure 5.1   Simple project evaluation process

A more comprehensive project evaluation will include evaluating different aspects of the project such as outcomes, project process and the impact of the project.

An evaluation of the project outcomes involves identifying whether or not the project achieved its objectives, whether it was on time and to budget, and the quality of its achievements. In addition any unexpected benefits or outcomes can be identified as well as any unwanted results.

Evaluating the project process involves assessing the:

- management, communication and reporting processes
- use of project management tools
- information systems
- documentation.

The impact of the project is the effect that the project process or outcomes have on individuals or groups. Peter Brophy (2002, p.2) lists the potential impact of projects as: 'may be positive or negative (though very often we focus on positive impacts); may be what was intended or something entirely different; may result in changed attitudes, behaviours, products (i.e. what an individual or group produces during or after interaction with the service); may be short or long term; may be critical or trivial'.

Brophy also describes different 'levels' of impact and gives the example that a project may result in any of the following impacts:

- hostility
- dismissive attitude
- none
- raising of awareness
- better information
- improved knowledge
- changed perception.

It is important to measure the impact of the project and to include this in the standard project evaluation process.

Design of the evaluation process

The design of the evaluation process is ideally carried out at the project planning stage as this will help ensure that all the required information is collected during the life of the project. It is useful to spend a little time considering the design principles of the evaluation process as these will shape the whole process. For example in the eLib project the evaluation process was based around six design principles, shown in Table 5.2.

Table 5.2 Evaluation design principles

Evaluation design principles	Key questions
Purposes of evaluation	What are the main purposes of evaluation?
Stakeholders	Who are the different actors who have a stake in the project and its evaluation?
Lifecycle	What evaluation activities are appropriate at different stages of the project life cycle?
Utilization	How will evaluation be integrated into the project?
User involvement	How will users be involved in evaluation?
Methods and techniques	What kinds of evaluation questions will be asked and what assessment methods are appropriate?

Adapted from Kelleher, Sommerlad and Stern (1996)

Once there is clarity about the design principles of the evaluation process it is important to think about the information requirements and this involves thinking about:

- Who needs the information?
- What information is required?
- How will it be obtained?
- Who are the most appropriate people to collect it?
- How will they collect this information?
- When will they collect this information?
- How will the information be analysed?
- How will it be presented to others?

Collecting information

There are a number of standard methods of collecting information, including the use of:

- project statistics
- project documentation
- project diary or log
- questionnaires
- interviews
- focus groups.

Project statistics typically will make up part of the evaluation process. They will vary depending on the specific project and may include figures such as:

- number of information and library units involved in the project
- number of staff involved in the project
- number of staff hours involved in the projects
- number of items processed
- number of hits on the website.

Project statistics are most easily collected if you know what information you require at the start of the project. This enables you to acquire this information as the project proceeds rather than be involved in a major information-collecting activity at the end of the project. If the latter happens it is possible that you may not be able to collect some of the statistics as they may no longer be available.

The *project documentation* and records all provide vital information and if the structure and format of these are agreed at the start of the project it can save a lot of time. Many project managers keep a project diary, which can be useful to help capture day-to-day information, ideas and thoughts that might otherwise be lost. Teams working on the project may keep their own log of their work, for example number of items processed each day, numbers of queries.

Questionnaires are a relatively simple method of collecting information but they are deceptively time consuming to design and analyse. They generally contain two types of question:

- Closed questions where there are a limited number of answers, e.g. yes/no, rating on a scale of 1–5.
- Open questions where the respondent has an opportunity to write their thoughts, idea or impressions, e.g. what do you think of Service X? How has project Y had an impact on your work?

Closed questions are relatively simple to analyse and process. While open questions often provide extremely useful information, this may be more challenging to evaluate. Questionnaires may be sent out to individuals via e-mail or post; alternatively individuals may be asked to complete them at service points or in meetings. Increasingly interactive questionnaires are included in online systems and services, and these provide another route for obtaining feedback. The advantages and disadvantages of questionnaires are summarized in Table 5.3:

Interviews are an extremely useful way of 'getting beneath the surface' and obtaining detailed information and views from people. As with questionnaires, interviews may involve open or closed questions and they may be structured (where the interviewer asks a set list of questions), semi-structured (where the interviewer provides some prompts or questions and then follows up individual responses) or unstructured interviews (where the respondent talks through their ideas and 'goes with the flow'. One major disadvantage with interviews is that they can be difficult to arrange as busy people may not want to give up their time. In addition, interviews can be time consuming to design, take part in and analyse.

The author has experimented with online interviews using conferencing or chat software. This appears to be a useful evaluation tool, particularly as the ensuing transcript is readable! However, this type of interview does demand that the individuals concerned have access to the technology and are comfortable with its use. Again, the advantages and disadvantages of interviews are summarized in Table 5.3.

Focus groups are groups of people who come together to discuss their views in a meeting which is facilitated by a researcher. The discussions in these meetings are frequently recorded on audio- or videotape and then analysed. Using a focus group means that the session may be structured, unstructured or semi-structured and individuals have the opportunity to 'spark' ideas off each other, which can lead to extremely rich and fruitful discussions. However, focus groups can be difficult to organize as many people don't have time to attend such a session. In addition they need careful facilitation so that the facilitator or session leader doesn't introduce bias and, finally, the results of these sessions can be quite time consuming to analyse. Again, their advantages and disadvantages are summarized in Table 5.3.

Table 5.3 Advantages and disadvantages of different data-gathering techniques

	Advantages	Disadvantages
Questionnaires	Relatively simple to disseminate. A number of different people can be involved in disseminating them and collecting them in.	May be time consuming to design and analyse. May be a low return as a result of individuals being unwilling to complete them.
Interviews	Provide in-depth information. New ideas or thoughts can be followed up.	May be time consuming to design and analyse. May be difficult to arrange.
Focus groups	Provide in-depth information. Individuals may 'spark off' ideas with each other. New ideas or thoughts can be followed up.	May be time consuming to design and analyse. Data collection methods, e.g. video-, audiotape, may be intrusive and put participants off. May be difficult to arrange. Need an experienced facilitator.

Analysing information

The project evaluation process involves analysing the information that you obtain and drawing conclusions from your findings. Quantitative information is best analysed using simple statistics and measures such as mean, mode, average and range. Information is often best presented using graphs and charts which enable the reader to quickly identify trends and charts. Qualitative information is often harder to analyse and the simplest approach is often to identify underlying themes and trends and then present them using a simple summary, perhaps supported by quotations. The selective use of relevant quotations can help reports to be interesting and they bring out more personal aspects of the experience.

Two useful sources of information on quantitative and qualitative research are Gorman and Clayton (2003) and Stephen and Hornby (1997).

Disseminating good practice

There are many different reasons for informing people about your project and its outcomes. With externally funded projects the sponsor often demands that you disseminate information about the project. This situation arises with national and international projects funded by organizations such as JISC and it is one of the ways that they ensure that the lessons learnt from your project are shared across the profession. It also enables your funder to demonstrate to their funder how they are spending their money! Other reasons for disseminating information about the project include sharing good practice among the profession, publicizing your ILS, personal satisfaction and career progression.

The main ways in which information about projects is disseminated is via reports, presentations, community events and websites. The following section outlines some basic ideas about disseminating information using these methods. Additional information on communication methods for library and information professionals is available from Sheldrick Ross and Dewdney (1998).

Report writing

Reports are a standard method of communicating information about projects. As mentioned earlier in this book, many project funders require written reports to be produced as part of the project outcomes and sometimes the parent body may require a written report. Written reports are useful as they provide detailed information about the project and its outcomes and they may be used by other information workers who wish to learn from people's experiences. This means that it is really useful to include information about the 'reality' of the project – what worked very well, what were the barriers to your work and what you would do differently next time. Project reports vary in size from two to three pages through to a whole book.

One of the key features about reports is their structure and while this varies from organization to organization all reports are likely to have a structure similar to the following:

- Title
- Author(s)
- Draft number and date
- Acknowledgements. This section will mention sponsors and other people whose help has been critical to the project.
- Executive summary. A summary of the report that presents all the key findings in an extremely concise manner.
- Introduction. A brief statement that outlines what the report is about, why it has been written, the scope of the report, and key issues.
- Background. This outlines the context of the project, e.g. organization, key issues. It may include reference to current practice and relevant literature.

- The project. An outline of the project and its key features. This section may cover issues such as funding, resourcing, use of project management tools, management issues.
- Outcomes of the project.
- Evaluation of the project.
- Implications for the future. This section may cover a range of implications such as staffing, training, premises, impact on other services, lessons learnt from the project.
- Recommendations for action
- Summary
- References
- Appendices.

A sample report structure is shown in Figure 5.2.

Title: Libraries & Learners in London (Baker and Hiscoe, 2003)

Final report
Date
Introduction
Aims and objectives
Timetable and milestones
Phase 1 – creation
Phase 2 – production
Phase 3 – operation
Further information
Challenges
Dissemination
Overall

Figure 5.2   Sample project report structure

Report writing involves a series of processes:

1 Identify your audience. Who are they, what do they hope to gain from reading your report?
2 Identify an outline structure for your report. If you are working on an externally funded report then check whether or not the sponsor has an in-house style with respect to the report structure and content. This information may be available in your contract or on the funder's website.
3 Collect information for the report. Start to organize this information under the headings.
4 Produce a first draft.
5 Ideally take a few days' break from report writing.
6 Return to the report and edit the draft.

7 Ask someone else to read the report and obtain their feedback. If you are working in a team you could ask everyone in the team to read it and give you feedback on the report.

8 Edit the report.

9 Re-read the report and edit for consistency, e.g. use of language, headings, references.

10 Once you are satisfied with the report it will need to be produced. This may involve:

a. producing a paper copy

b. producing a web-based version.

At this stage you may want to involve the services of a graphic designer to ensure that the report is visually attractive.

11 Once you are satisfied with the report, ensure that it is disseminated. This may involve:

a. Sending copies to sponsors, stakeholders and project team members

b. Handing out copies at meetings and conferences

c. Sending copies out to other interested parties

d. Disseminating it via the project website.

Community events

One way of disseminating information about your project is to organize a community event where the project is presented to a local audience. Community events may involve bringing together library and information unit customers, sponsors and library and information workers. Special guests, for example celebrities, authors or local dignitaries, may be invited too.

Example   Learning Development Unit Open Days and Events

The Learning and Development Unit (LDU) of the Information Services Department, University of Birmingham, regularly organizes open days and events to disseminate the outcomes of their projects within the University and also to the wider community. The LDU is involved in a wide range of projects concerned with learning and teaching and involving information services and academic staff. The dissemination events typically involve a range of keynote presentations, demonstrations and poster sessions, accompanied by refreshments. In addition the LDU regularly circulates newsletters about their activities. Their website can be visited on www.bham.ac.uk/informationservices/ldu.

Example   CIAO Project Model

'CIAO can be described as an intensive after-school community technology program requiring 5–6 hours per week for the school year. CIAO's aim was to foster teen civic engagement by giving the teen participants the skills they needed to help a community organization as it developed a web presence. Thus students needed to increase their knowledge of the community and develop a range of technology skills. To do this, participants were required to spend one afternoon a week and a Saturday morning engaged in active learning and site development. . . . The two-year CIAO program, funded in part by the W.K. Kellogg Foundation, met at the main branch of the Flint Public Library. In the program's first year, participants took part in a series of projects to expand their computer skills with a focus on Internet publishing (software applications and digital image handling); CIAO participants, high school youth, met leaders from the local community and worked in teams to create community-valued resources. During the second year, the program was scaled back from thirty high school students (and six UM graduate student coaches) to twelve high school students and two high school student mentors, graduates of the first year program. The project incorporated the skill sets of several Flint Public Library staff members and two University of Michigan School of Information graduate students. As an integral part of the Flint project, Flint Public Library staff held periodic public celebrations designed to foster pride, self-confidence and presentation skills of the participants as well as to have them exhibit their work. Students and staff invited parents, non-profit organizations, local community leaders, and the local news media including the local television station to these events that were always accompanied by refreshments. Students had opportunities to present their work briefly to the entire group and demonstrate it at one of the computer stations in the lab. In addition, a few students had the opportunity to make public presentations at venues sponsored by the W.K. Kellogg Foundation.' (Anon, 2002)

Conference papers and presentations

Conference papers and presentations at meetings offer an important way in which information can be disseminated throughout the profession. Calls for papers are regularly circulated in the professional literature and also via e-mail discussion lists. If you are interested in presenting your project at a conference then the first step is to identify an appropriate conference.

Read the call for papers and check that your work will fit into the conference theme. If you are uncertain as to the suitability of your work contact the organizer and discuss it with them. The next step is normally to send in an abstract or summary of your proposed paper and presentation. This abstract will need to reach the conference organizers by the closing date and the abstract will be sent to a reviewer or the conference committee who will decide whether or not to accept your paper. If it is accepted then you may be asked to write and return a completed paper by a set date which is normally a month or two before the actual conference. This gives the organizers time to publish the conference papers, either in a printed proceedings or via a website. Many conferences don't require a detailed paper but may ask for a copy of your PowerPoint presentation either before or during the conference; again, this may be uploaded on to the conference web page.

The organizers will give you a time and location for your presentation and they will normally ask you for your equipment requirements.

Preparation

The more prepared you are, the less worried you'll be.
The more prepared you are, the more effective you'll be.
The less prepared you are, the more worried you'll be.
The more worried you are, the less effective you'll be.
If you are going to be more effective, it's important not to worry.
If you don't prepare, you will worry.

(Kalish, 1997)

A well prepared presentation that is delivered with enthusiasm is always well received by an audience. If you are involved in presentations then it is important to spend time on preparation and also thinking about how you will deliver the presentation.

The benefits of planning and preparing your presentation include:

• It gives you confidence so that you won't dry up.
• It focuses your thinking on the needs of the audience.
• It helps you to be prepared with appropriate audiovisual aids.
• It helps you to anticipate possible problems and develop contingency plans.
• You are less likely to make basic errors during the presentation.
• It looks professional.

Being prepared involves thoroughly researching and designing your presentation. You will need to research your audience and answer questions such as:

• Who is the audience?
• How many people will be there?
• What are they likely to want from the presentation?
• What is their knowledge about the subject?

You will also need to think about the venue, for example the size of the room and the availability of facilities such as IT-based presentation hardware and software. Nowadays the majority of presentations are prepared and presented using software such as MS PowerPoint and, if it is not something that you are familiar with, it is well worthwhile spending time getting to grips with this type of package. It is also worthwhile taking a set of slides on acetate as back-up just in case there are problems with the technology on the day. It pays to double check the IT facilities and the compatibility with your own resources. For example if you have stored your presentation on a USB stick (a removable memory device) then you need to ensure that the computer you will use during the presentation is able to take a USB stick and also that you are able to gain access to the necessary port. In some lecture theatres computer equipment is boxed in for security purposes and there is no access to the back of the hardware.

When you are preparing the presentation you will need to structure it. The simplest structure involves dividing your presentation into three parts: introduction, main section, conclusion. This is shown in the examples structure given below.

Example   Presentation structure

Introduction.
> Introduce self. Acknowledgements. Give a very brief introduction to the topic/theme for the day.

Background. The organizational or ILS context of the project. The reasons and rationale for the project.

The project. This could be organized around headings such as: Funding, Staffing, Use of ICT.

Project outcomes

Project evaluation

Lessons learnt for next time

Summary

Any questions

Close and thank the audience.

Another approach to planning a presentation is to use the project planning cycle as the framework as shown below.

Example   Another presentation structure

Introduction.
> Introduce self. Acknowledgements. Give a very brief introduction to the topic/theme for the day.

Background. The organizational or ILS context of the project.

The project
> Initiation
>
> Analysis
>
> Planning
>
> Implementation
>
> Evaluation

Summary

Any questions

Close and thank the audience.

Rehearsals are best carried out in front of an audience, perhaps friends and colleagues at work. If no audience is available then consider video- or audiotaping yourself. Some people (including the author) rehearse in front of family members and pets!

The presentation

On the day of the presentation make sure that you allow yourself plenty of time to find the venue and check that all the equipment is set up and working. If you are taking part in a conference that you haven't attended before or if the audience is unfamiliar to you then spend a little time attending other people's sessions as this will give you a feel for the event and people's expectations.

The best presentations are those that start with a strong and enthusiastic introduction. Vary the tone and pace of your voice during the presentation to help make it more interesting. Move around and use hand and arm gestures as a way of making your presentation lively but avoid the trap of repetitive movements, which can be distracting to the audience. Make sure that the presentation ends on a positive note and does not fade away.

Questions and discussions from the audience are an important part of any presentation. As presenter it is worthwhile thinking about how you will handle them. Do you want to take questions throughout the presentation or leave them until the end? If you are not an experienced presenter then leaving questions until the end tends to be easier as it means that you are not knocked off your course during the presentation. Whatever you decide to do, let the audience know at the start of the presentation. Control the number of questions answered by the use of phrases such as 'There is time for one more question'.

Sometimes challenging situations arise during presentations. Table 5.4 provides some simple guidelines for handling common situations.

Table 5.4 Managing challenging situations during presentations

Situation	Possible responses
Someone asks a question that you can't answer.	Be honest. Say that you can't answer the question. Ask them to let you have their name and contact details at the end of the session and say that you will contact them after the conference.
One person takes over the question session and 'hogs' the time.	State that you want to give other people the opportunity to ask questions and that if that person wants to you will meet up with them after the presentation.
Two members of the audience start to argue with each other.	Don't take sides. If appropriate, suggest that they agree to disagree. Find some common ground. Move on to another topic.
Someone challenges the fundamental basis of your project, e.g. if the project is externally funded then they suggest that the money would have been better spent on another project (probably one that they support).	Don't get into an argument. State that you were sponsored to complete this project and that is the focus of your presentation. If they want to discuss the ways in which your sponsor distributes grants then perhaps they should contact the sponsor.

At the end of the presentation remember to thank the audience for their time and participation.

After the presentation

Ask for feedback from colleagues in the audience and read the evaluation forms. Use this information to help you to improve your presentations in future. Make contact with those people whom you promised to contact. This is very important as being part of a professional network is an important part of professional life and it helps support career development.

Websites

Many projects develop and maintain a website as this helps to disseminate information about the project and its activities. If you are involved in a project that decides to market itself using a website then you will need to include staff time in your project plan for this activity and, in addition, you will need to ensure that you have access to people with web design and development skills. Phil Bradley (2002) provides a readable and useful guide to 'Getting and staying noticed on the web'.

Typical project websites contain the following:

- home page
- site map and help facilities
- outline of project aims and outcomes
- details of project staff – names, contact details and (perhaps) photographs
- details of project funders and sponsors
- project events – a diary, often with online booking facilities, e.g. for dissemination events or workshops
- project publications – a list of project publications, often with the facility to download these items in PDF format
- project resources – details of project resources e.g. sample materials, publications
- project links – links to other relevant websites, e.g. similar or related projects, project funders, parent organizations
- project contact details – addresses, phone numbers, map, online query form.

In addition some project websites include discussion groups and/or conference or chat rooms (see Chapter 7).

If you are using a website to market your project then it is worthwhile including a counter on the relevant page. This will enable you to monitor and measure how many people are accessing the site.

Getting your message across

Jenny Rowley (2003) provides some useful advice on branding ILS websites, which is equally relevant to project websites. She defines a brand mark as 'a recognisable symbol that identifies an organisation or product, and links together different marketing communications from one organisation' (Rowley, 2003, p.45). In other words, branding is about a recognizable symbol and the messages and style that go with it. For example, an ILS project might be concerned with digitizing maps and their brand might be a symbol of local maps accompanied by messages that encourage access to scholars. Another project might be concerned with storytelling for the under-tens and their brand might be a book logo associated with messages of fun and inclusiveness. In speaking of ILS websites Rowley says that 'many sites are bland, others are confusing, not necessarily in their design and layout, but often in the messages that are communicated. With increasing numbers of users interacting with library services remotely, libraries need to think about their relationship building through their website. Reflection on branding is a good starting point.'

Rowley (2003) identifies website elements that communicate brand values and messages and identifies the following important features:

- *Overall image.* What is the overall impression that you want to make with your website? The combination of layout, colours, images, text and shapes will send a message about your project.
- *Text.* What style of language are you going to use in your website? How will you encourage people to read about and engage with your project? How will you ensure that the style is friendly and accessible? Will you use quotations, e.g. from satisfied users or staff? How will the text be presented? What typescript will be used?
- *Images.* Pictures are often used to enhance websites and portray a project. What type of images do you want to use? Images of illuminated texts put across a very different image from photographs of children.
- *Colour.* The colours that you use in your website will send a message about the project. Many project websites have to follow the corporate colours of their parent organizations. If you are involved in selecting the colours then consider the messages that individual colours put across. Think about how the colours, images and text all come together. You want to project an integrated image of your project rather than a set of competing visual images.
- *Shapes.* Most websites contain an array of shapes, e.g. shapes of buttons or menu option items. Different shapes present very different images and you need to consider which types of shapes will support the general message that you want to portray.

Navigation

The website needs to be simple to navigate so that individuals looking at it know where they are, how they got there and where they can move to next. It is important that the materials are organized in a logical way and that guiding is available. The following facilities are typically used to help people navigate websites:

- home page with site map
- search tools
- help facility
- headings
- menu of contents
- index
- glossary
- hotlinks
- bookmarks.

Usability

It is really important that the website is readable and easy to use. There is nothing worse than being faced with indigestible chunks of dense reading material in a very small font. Factors that need to be considered include the following:

- Text is legible against the background.
- An appropriate font style and size are used.
- Text is surrounded by sufficient space – 'white space'.
- Text is chunked into appropriate sizes, e.g. 5–6 points per chunk.
- Long pages include a table of contents and a 'back to top' button.
- Lists and bullet points are used rather than large blocks of text.
- Horizontal scrolling is minimized.
- Accessibility is maximized, e.g. by providing large font versions, text of audiotapes.

Introducing text, sounds and images

It is relatively simple to use software packages to integrate a wide range of materials into a website such as:

- document files
- PowerPoint files
- audio files
- image files
- video files
- animation files.

Document files using PDF (Portable Document Format) are created and read in Adobe Acrobat. They are widely used as a means of distributing documents on the internet. PDF file links allow content to be displayed files in a new window. Images that have been created outside Word and are held in .gif or .jpg files can be included in the document. Images can be included as a background as well as in the foreground of the screen. Audio files can be played as clickable links or background audio which starts as soon as a page is loaded or on the closedown of a section. Director or Shockwave movies can be made in Macromedia Director and Shockwave (.dcr and .swf files) and then included in the content.

There is a balance to be achieved between providing a multimedia presentation and providing a website that is accessible and quick to access. It is important to consider the needs of diverse users, for example people who have impaired hearing, and to provide alternative formats, such as scripts to accompany audio clips and captions on video clips. This topic is explored in detail in the next section.

Make your website accessible

Juliet Owen (2003, p.48) provides detailed guidance on website accessibility which is about 'people being able to get and use web content with ease'. Although discussions about website accessibility focus on the needs of users with disabilities the design of accessible websites means improving the online experiences of all web users. She quotes the World Wide Web Consortium (W3C) who describe the context of many users as follows:

- they may not be able to see, hear, move or process some types of information easily or at all
- they may have difficulty reading or comprehending text
- they may not have or be able to use a key board or mouse
- they may have a text-only screen, a small screen, or a slow internet connection
- they may not speak or understand fluently the language in which the documentation is written
- they may be in a situation where their eyes, ears, or hands are busy or are hampered
- they may have an early version of a browser, a different browser entirely, a voice browser, or a different operating system.

Owen (2003, p.49) provides a summary of quick tips from the W3C guidelines:

- Images & animations. Use the alt attribute to describe the function of each visual.
- Image maps. Use the client-side map and text for hot spots.
- Multimedia. Provide captioning and transcripts for audio, and descriptions of video.
- Hypertext links. Use text that makes sense when read out of context. For example, avoid 'click here'.
- Page organisation. Use headings, lists and consistent structure.

- Graphs & charts. Summarise or use the longdesc attribute.
- Scripts, applets, & plug-ins. Provide alternative content in case active features are inaccessible and unsupported.
- Frames. Use the noframes element and meaningful titles.
- Tables. Make line-by-line reading sensible. Summarise.
- Check your work. Validate. Use tools, checklists and guidelines. (www.w3.org/TR/WCAG).

Examples of accessible media rich materials can be found at http://ncam.wgbh.org/richmedia/examples/index.php.

Further information on this topic is available from The Web Accessibility Initiative at www.w3.org/TR/WAI-WEBCONTENT/.

Summary

This chapter outlines the project evaluation process, which may range from a quick and informal evaluation involving the project team through to an in-depth study involving a wide range of stakeholders. The results of the project evaluation process may be used by the ILS and their parent organization, stakeholders, funders and the library and information profession as a whole. It provides a means by which projects and ILS can be marketed, good practice shared and lessons learnt. A wide range of dissemination methods are used including reports, community events, conference papers and presentations, and websites. It is important that these are designed to meet the needs of the audience. Websites are a very common way of keeping people informed about a project and its outcomes and the chapter concludes with ideas about their design, including design for accessibility.

References

Anon. (2002) *Public Library After-School Community Technology Programs*, Michigan, University of Michigan, www.si.umich.edu/libhelp/toolkit/collectCombinedFAReport.html.

Baker, S. and Hiscoe, M. (2003) *Libraries and Learners in London – Final Report, February 2003*, www.bl.uk/concord/pdf.files/llilfinal.pdf.

Bradley, P. (2002) *Getting and Staying Noticed on the Web*, London, Facet Publishing.

Brophy, P. (2002) *The Evaluation of Public Library Online Services: measuring impact*, The People's Network Workshop Series Issue Papers, 1, www.peoplesnetwork.gov.

Gorman, G. E. and Clayton, P. (2003) *Qualitative Research for the Information Profession: a practical handbook*, London, Facet Publishing.

Kalish, K. (1997) *How to Give a Terrific Presentation*, New York, American Management Association.

Kelleher, J., Sommerlad, E. and Stern, E. (1996) *Evaluation of the Electronic Libraries Programme. Guidelines for eLib project evaluation*, The Tavistock Institute, www.ukoln.ac.uk/services/elib/papers/tavistock/evaluation-guide/.

Owen, J. (2003) Making Your Website Accessible, *Library & Information Update*, **2** (1), 48–9.

Ross, C. S. and Dewdney, P. (1998) *Communicating Professionally*, 2nd edn, London, Facet Publishing.

Rowley, J. (2003) Branding your Library Website, *Library & Information Update*, **2** (2), 45.

Stephen, P. and Hornby, S. (1997) *Simple Statistics for Library and Information Professionals*, 2nd edn, Library Association Publishing.

6

The money side of projects

Introduction

The ability to understand and manage the money side of projects is an essential skill for all project managers. Although some ILS projects are carried out within normal departmental budgets, many projects are funded by external sources. This means that many information workers become involved in obtaining external funding and then managing a budget. The focus of this chapter is funding and obtaining funds from external sources. In addition, the chapter covers current approaches to funding, external sources of funding, bidding and tendering for projects, managing the finances, and audits.

Appendix A contains a glossary of common terms relating to the money side of projects.

Current approaches to funding

The last ten years have seen the rise of a competitive bidding culture in which different organizations bid for public or private sector funds. Funding is available from a wide range of sources including international organizations, the European Union, central and regional governments, businesses, charitable and other special funds, and individual donors.

This bidding culture is driven by a range of factors. First, public funding has been reduced. Secondly, there is a belief that bidding promotes better use of resources, increased accountability and creativity. Sometimes there can also be a desire to fund and support particular ways of working, or to facilitate cross-organizational and/or cross-sectoral approaches. Finally, the integration of a diverse range of organizations, departments and services can play its part.

Today in the UK and other countries a wide range of projects on themes as varied as ICT developments, social inclusion needs, improvement of storage to meet standards, extending access, digitization of resources, lifelong learning, information provision, remote services, for example to rural communities, upgrading and relocating accommodation are supported by external funding.

The work of Parker et al. (2001) demonstrates the current importance of the bidding culture in public sector library and information work. In their research report *The Bidding Culture and Local Government: effects on the development of public libraries, museums and archives* they state that 'Bidding for funds, especially additional monies, is now widely accepted in the archives, libraries and museums sectors as part of the everyday management agenda.' Their findings indicate that 73% of archives, libraries and museums submitted bids for at least one or two major projects during the study period and that only 3% of libraries had not submitted bids for projects worth over £10,000. They found that during 1997–2000

> there has been a marked rise in bidding activity in all three sectors. This growth is in part attributable to increased experience, expertise and confidence in bidding, as well as being driven by political necessity. For many, engagement in the bidding culture is the only viable means by which to develop and improve services, given existing deficiencies in core funding (Parker et al., 2001, p.2).

External sources of funding

Keeping up to date with possible sources of funding is a challenging task. The purpose of this section is to alert the reader to the wide range of funding sources that are currently available in the UK rather than to attempt to provide a comprehensive list of all the potential sources of funding. Currently there is a diverse range of sources of funding and the types and availability of funds is constantly changing. Funding opportunities change over time as the priorities of funding organizations change along with their access to funds. This means that anyone who is considering bidding for funding must do extensive research to identify current sources of funding and their up-to-date detailed requirements. Many information workers make use of specialists who will provide up-to-date information and advice on funding matters. For example, local authorities typically employ specialist staff with expertise in funding and funding applications in their economic development units, while universities often have a centralized research and development department that provides access to this type of specialist information. In addition, individual consultants working in this field offer their services and expertise in funding applications too.

For information and library workers based in the UK funding is available from the following sources:

- central and regional government agencies
- European Union funds
- local authorities
- National Lottery
- trusts and foundations
- businesses
- individuals.

Stuart Brewer (2002) identified over 38 funding streams in his report entitled *Overview of Funding Streams for Libraries and Learning in England*, including:

- A2A (Access to Archives) Programme
- Adult and Community Learning Fund
- Arts and Humanities Research Board
- Arts Council funding: Invest to Save Budget
- Arts Lottery funding
- Awards for All (England): Lottery grants for local groups
- Awards Research Resources in Medical History
- Basic Skills Agency programmes
- British Library Co-operation and Partnership Programme
- BT Lifelong Learning Awards
- Capital Modernisation Fund
- Community Fund
- European Union, e.g. European Social Fund
- Heritage Lottery Fund
- Higher Education Funding Council for England (HEFCE)
- Joint Information Systems Committee (JISC)
- Laser Foundation
- Learning and Skills Councils
- Local Public Service Agreements
- Millennium Awards Scheme
- National Manuscripts Conservation Trust
- Neighbourhood Renewal Funding
- Neighbourhood Support Fund
- New Learning Opportunities Awards
- New Opportunities Fund
- Paul Hamlyn Trust
- Private Finance Initiative
- Reading Families
- Research Support Libraries Programme (RSLP)
- Single Regeneration Budget
- Sir Jules Thorn Charitable Trust
- Union Learning Fund
- Wired-up Communities
- Wolfson Foundation

Working in partnership

Finance is often a key driver for partnership working as this frequently attracts funding in a way that working as an independent library or information department or agency will not. The finances will often drive the project as monies may be available and must be used up within a specified time period. Project managers are increasingly asked to lead project teams that involve ILS and perhaps other staff from organizations either within their sector or across sectors.

The appearance of 'calls to tender' sometimes results in frenzied activities as individuals and their organizations attempt to find appropriate partners and establish a partnership that will enable them to successfully bid for funds. Partners may be sought within the same sector or in different sectors and many projects require cross-sector and multi-professional working. In some cases the matchmaking and the marriage may take place over a matter of weeks resulting in the living out of the old adage 'Marry in haste and repent at leisure'. Individuals and organizations with a track record in successfully gaining external funds normally have well established networks including potential partners and this means that the relationships essential for successful funding applications and project working are already firmly established and can be demonstrated in the funding application. This suggests that for ILS that are new to the bidding culture it is worthwhile starting to build up appropriate networks and contacts well before the appearance of any calls to tender. Working in partnership is considered in more detail in Chapter 9.

Bidding and tendering for projects

Experience of the bidding culture suggests that it can be an extremely time-consuming and resource-intensive process. Reading all the relevant paperwork can be heavy going and writing a succinct bid that meets the needs of the funding organization as well as the ILS and its stakeholders can engulf vast swathes of time. Information workers need expertise or access to expertise in writing bids. Many public sector organizations, for example local authorities and universities, employ specialist staff whose sole remit is keeping up to date with funding organizations and their requirements, and providing help and support in writing bids. This can exclude smaller and independent organizations who may contract the services of a consultant to develop their funding application. The actual bidding process producers 'winners and losers' – for those that are unsuccessful in obtaining a bid after they have invested much time and effort it can be an extremely demoralizing experience. For the winner they may suddenly find that they need to get a project up and running in a matter of weeks, often while they are still fully engaged in their full-time job role.

Although access to external funds provides ILS with wide-ranging opportunities and the ability to develop new and innovative services, there are disadvantages to working on externally funded projects. Thake (2001) identifies a range of operational difficulties with respect to funding and reporting regimes and suggests that these can create chronic financial insecurity as well as a major administrative burden. Changes in policy at the national and European levels also means that for many externally funded projects the rules and procedures may change at regular intervals, adding to the already heavy workload of project managers and workers. In addition the focus of funding is often on outcomes rather than processes and this may put pressure on managers to meet the outcomes at a cost of setting up a sustainable process. For project managers who have obtained funding for their projects from a variety of sources, the administrative burden of managing the different agents' requirements can be immense. Other challenges to working on externally funded projects include the frequent requirement to work in partnership (explored in Chapter 9) and the employment of ILS staff on externally funded projects (explored in Chapter 10).

CASE STUDY   Darwin Correspondence Project

The Darwin Correspondence Project is a scholarly, non-profit-making undertaking to publish the definitive edition of all the letters written by and to Charles Darwin. This is a long-lived project that started in 1974. It is a good case study to include here as it demonstrates the following characteristics: a project funded from a multiplicity of different sources, and success in a changing funding climate. Information on this case study has been obtained from the project website www.lib.cam.ac.uk/Departments/Darwin/ and also a presentation given by Alison Pearn (2002) at a conference entitled 'The Bidding Culture: CURL Task Force on Staffing Resources' (www.curl.ac.uk/about/biddingculture.html).

> 'The Project was founded in 1974 by a Cambridge zoologist, Sydney Smith, and an American scholar, Fred Burkhardt, who wanted something to do in his retirement. Fred is still the Project's Senior Editor and will celebrate his 90th birthday later this year. We know of around 15000 letters in total which Darwin exchanged with nearly 2000 correspondents. The originals are now scattered through roughly 200 institutions and private collections in at least 20 countries around the world. The single largest collection is in Cambridge University Library, and although the Project's director and senior editor are based in the US, most of the salaried staff are based in Cambridge, and today the Project is jointly managed by the Library and the American Council of Learned Societies. The Cambridge team currently has 5 full time editors, 3 part timers – a clerical assistant, a research associate and a computer associate – all paid from UK sources, and a sixth editor paid from US funds. We also currently have funding for a computer consultant to work on a specific product' (Pearn, 2003, slide 3).

The project presents some unique features in addition to being a joint UK/USA venture and being jointly managed by the American Council of Learned Societies and Cambridge University Library. It has offices in three locations: Cambridge University Library, Bennington, Vermont, at the home of the project's founder and director, Frederick Burkhardt, and Virginia Polytechnic Institute and State University, Blacksburg, Virginia. The project involves bidding for the costing of core staff who are based at CUL with a team of volunteers at Bennington. The project has a broad-based appeal and crosses a number of different communities, for example scientific, historical, it has a very clear focus, i.e. the publication of the letters of Charles Darwin, and it has so-called 'brand recognition' as both Charles Darwin and his work are well known around the world.

Alison Pearn describes some of the positives and negatives involved in this type of project work: 'being a long running project with a proven product may mean we have to explain ourselves less, but it also means we have to combat donor fatigue, and work much harder to convince people that what we do hasn't gone stale to maintain and convey our own enthusiasm.' In addition she says that 'Most donors are uncomfortable about such a distant end point – currently estimated at 2024.' Also the project members are 'victims of our own success – have built up a patchwork of funding but that brings its own problems' and this is explored below.

The Darwin Correspondence Project is funded by a wide range of individuals and organizations which include government agencies, learned societies and also private charitable foundations. These represent a diverse range of interests from the arts and humanities to science and medicine. The following list illustrates the diverse range of sources that make up the project funding base.

UK and Europe
- Arts and Humanities Research Board
- British Academy
- British Ecological Society
- Isaac Newton Trust
- Jephcott Charitable Trust
- Natural Environment Research Council
- Pilgrim Trust
- the late Miss Kathleen Mary Smith
- Royal Society of London
- Stifterverband für die Deutsche Wissenschaft
- Wellcome Trust
- Wilkinson Charitable Foundation

USA
- Alfred P. Sloan Foundation
- Andrew W. Mellon Foundation
- the late Dr Bern Dibner
- the late Miss Mary S. Hopkins
- National Endowment for the Humanities
- National Science Foundation
- Pew Charitable Trusts

This project clearly demonstrates how a specific project may gain funding from a wide range of sources, sometimes called a 'patchwork' of funding. The Darwin project team obviously have a track record in identifying and obtaining new sources of funding as well as maintaining existing sources. This process is clearly a complex one as it requires the project team to be meeting the differing needs of diverse funding bodies and to be working on different timelines for different grants. Their funding patchwork in 2002 is summarized below; it shows that the project manager must manage a number of different start and end dates for project funds:

Royal Society	Oct. 2001–Nov. 2002
British Academy	Apr. 2002–March 2003
NERC	Oct. 1999–Sept. 2003
BES	Feb. 2001–Jan. 2004
NEH (and Mellon)	Aug. 2002–July 2005
Wellcome	Oct. 2001–Sept. 2006
NSF	Apr. 2002–March 2007

The process of gaining funding varies from funder to funder and Pearn describes two contrasting examples of funding applications:

- The Wellcome Trust provided two five-year grants which gave long-term funding for core salaries. The route to each of these grants was different and involved a lengthy and demanding process. She writes, 'We were asked for more information. We were asked for a business plan – rather suddenly. We tried to see all this as an opportunity to strengthen both our case and our personal relationship with the members of the committee. And the good news is that they wanted us to succeed – they wanted to give us the chance to do well.'
- The Arts and Humanities Research Board (AHRB) provided relatively short-term funding for a discrete sub-project and this involved a relatively simple application process.

Alison Pearn identifies some of the challenges of multi-source funding. It can be an extremely time-consuming process as it involves identifying potential funders, engaging in the application process and writing detailed applications. As we have seen, working on a project that is funded by different grants means that you are likely to be dealing with a range of different timescales as each grant will have different start and end dates. In addition they may have different reporting requirements and demand different types of written reports. This increases the workload on the project manager. Another challenge of multi-source funding is the impact on project staff as it can create insecurity and instability, and inequalities may arise because of funding from different sources. Finally, the project manager needs to meet the needs of 'many masters' and this is an additional pressure. These issues relating to project workers and the project manager are explored in more detail in Chapters 10 and 11.

The bidding process

The bidding process is summarized in Figure 6.1. The first stage is the identification of a potential project; most ILS managers have existing or potential projects that may be used as the focus of a bidding process. These projects may have been identified during the strategic planning process within the ILS or may have evolved during the day-to-day work within a unit or in response to a particular problem or challenge. It is useful to write down the basic project idea as a project brief (see Chapter 2 for the structure and content of project briefs). It is really important that the brief includes a clear statement of project aims and outcomes and this may be refined as you work through the application process.

Summary of the bidding process
1   Identifying a potential project and starting work on project brief.
2   Identifying a potential source of funding.
3   Obtaining the necessary documentation.
4   Checking funders' requirements and criteria.
5   Checking with parent organization that this meets their aims.
6   Identifying a senior manager who will support the funding application.
7   Identifying a single individual who will be responsible for the project.
8   Carrying out research within the sector.
9   Carrying out research within the bidding organization.
10   Setting up or calling together a bidding team.
11   Producing a draft funding application.
12   Checking out queries with the funding organization.
13   Obtaining feedback and guidance from colleagues.
14   Editing and re-drafting the funding application.
15   Obtaining approval from own organization to send off the funding application.
16   Submitting the funding application within the timescale identified by the funding organization.
17   Receiving outcome of selection process.
18   If successful then rejoicing and starting project. If unsuccessful obtaining feedback from the funding organization and using it to help you become successful in your next application.

Figure 6.1   Summary of the bidding process

Initial research

The next stage is to identify potential sources of funding and, as suggested earlier in this chapter, this often requires considerable research. Once a potential source of funding is identified then you will need to obtain the documentation that outlines their funding programme(s) and requirements. Increasingly this documentation is only available via the internet and many funding organizations require the submission of electronic applications for funding. If you do obtain the documentation from the funding organization's website it is worthwhile monitoring the website at regular intervals as this means that you can pick up any additional information, for example more detailed explanations of their requirements, changes in submission dates, etc.

Once a potential source of funding is identified then it is vital to check the 'small print' and to ensure that you and your project will fit into the funder's requirements. Otherwise you may find that you are wasting time preparing a project bid for a funder who would not consider your application. If you are uncertain about their requirements then contact the funding organization, for example by phone or e-mail. Many funders organize special meetings or launches for new funding opportunities and these are well worth attending as they will give you an opportunity to find out more about the funder and what they are looking for.

You need to ensure that the proposed project fits into your own organization's or department's aims and objectives. This will help to ensure that if successful you will have support from within your own organization for the project. As mentioned in an earlier chapter, it is vital to gain support for your project from senior managers. Initially 'selling' your idea to one manager is often a good strategy and this can then be followed up by ensuring that the project proposal is discussed and (hopefully) supported by the senior team. You will need to identify someone who is going to take responsibility for putting together the funding application.

The basis of all good funding applications is research and you will need to demonstrate to the funding organization that your application is based on knowledge of current good practice. Many funding applications require you to demonstrate your knowledge of your current context and the ways in which your project will make a difference. This means being aware of relevant current government policy and activities within your particular sector (e.g. public library, higher education), area of interest (e.g. digitization, metadata, information literacy) and across the profession as a whole. This research will enable you to link your application to current thinking and activities, and it will help you to identify gaps that your project might fill. In addition it will help you to develop the appropriate language for the funding application.

Some organizations, for example many universities and some public sector organizations, have an organizational structure that includes teams of people who will work with you in putting together your bid. They will be able to advise you on what is required for your application. Other organizations don't have this type of structure and some people find it helpful to put together a team of people who will take overall responsibility for the funding application. This team may include the person with overall responsibility for producing the application, individuals who are interested in and enthusiastic about the potential project, technical staff, finance staff and potential project champions.

You will also need to carry out research on your proposed project within your organization. The purpose of this research is to start thinking through some of the practical aspects of the project. It will answer questions such as:

- Who will become involved in the project?
- Where will the project take place?
- Is there an enabling infrastructure?
  — Is there an appropriate administrative infrastructure?
  — Is there an appropriate ICT infrastructure?
  — Are there appropriate financial systems?

Initial meetings may be held with appropriate directors and managers, for example the human resource manager, finance director, administrative manager. In these meetings you may want to show them the project brief and explain the basic ideas behind the project. Find out what you will need to do to put the project in place. For example, if it takes your organization six months to recruit a new member of staff this has implications for the project application.

Costing

Costing the project is a relatively straightforward activity. You will need to identify all the likely costs and present them in a suitable manner. Many organizations have their own sets of guidelines and rules for costing projects and it is worthwhile contacting the finance department before you start this stage. The list of headings which you will need to consider is shown below:

- staff
- durable equipment
- software
- consumables
- printed materials
- subscriptions
- external assistance, e.g. consultant, trainers
- printing
- travel and subsistence
- miscellaneous
- VAT.

Staffing is likely to be a major cost. As we saw in Chapter 3, it is important to calculate this using the following type of standard equations:

Daily rate = (annual salary + on-costs)/Working days

Working = Days in year – (annual leave + weekends + training days + statutory
days per　　　　　　　　　　　　　　　　　　　days + sick days)
year

$$= 365 - (20 + 104 + 4 + 11 + 10) = 216 \text{ days per annum.}$$

The on-costs are the costs to the organization of employing a member of staff. This is likely to consist of employer-related National Insurance contributions and pension contributions, typically 20% of the gross salary. Many organizations also charge an overhead for externally funded projects and this may be as much as 20%. This takes the on-costs to 40%. It is important to know the rules of your own organization before calculating the staff costs. If your project is going to last more than a year then any likely pay rises (e.g. cost of living or performance-related pay rises) will need to be included in the costings. Note that the number of working days that a full-time team member will be working on the project is only 220 days per annum.

　　The other project costs will need to be worked out and included in your project plan. An important detail is whether or not you can claim VAT on purchases. The rules for VAT are complicated and also change over time so you are advised to obtain up-to-date specialist advice on this subject, for example from your finance department.

Some funding organizations ask for a business plan and this is another name for the project budget. In a business plan you would outline projected costs, anticipated income and cash-flow projections e.g. income and expenditure on a monthly basis.

The draft application

The next step is to produce an initial draft funding application, which is a key stage in the funding application process. This draft application will need to be circulated and feedback obtained. Then the draft will be worked on and polished until it completely matches the requirements of the funding organization. This is a lengthy process and the draft application will go through many iterations before it is ready for submission. Questions or issues that arise during this feedback process and meetings of the bidding team need to be taken to the funding organization. The more clarity that you have about their expectations the more likely that you are to meet them.

Obtaining feedback and guidance from colleagues is an important part of the bidding process as it will help you to sharpen up your application and mean that you include a range of ideas and perspectives. Send copies of your draft bid to colleagues (both within and external to your organization) and ask them for feedback. If you have specific queries or concerns then it is sometimes appropriate to use an e-mail discussion list as a means of obtaining further information or advice. However, this does mean that you may allow your competitors to know your plans. Remember that if individuals are generous with their time and experience in helping you to put together your bid it is important to thank them and also to repay their work 'in kind' at a later date.

Continue editing the funding application. Keep checking back to the requirements of the funding organization to ensure that your application doesn't drift and develop in new directions (that don't meet the requirements of the funding organization) as time goes by.

Submitting the application

Once the funding application is ready you will also need to obtain approval from your own manager and/or organization to send it off. Many funding organizations require that the funding application is supported by a statement of commitment from a senior member of staff, for example RSLP (the Research Support Library Programme) require a statement of support from the vice-chancellor, director or principal of the organization(s) submitting a funding application.

It is vital that you submit the funding application within the timescale identified by the funding organization. This sounds obvious, but it is worth knowing that with many large national or international funding processes applications that are one minute late will not be considered. If you are submitting your application electronically it is always a good idea to submit it 24 hours before the closing date as this will provide time to sort out any unexpected technical difficulties. Keep the receipt or acknowledgement of your application.

Different funding organizations will inform applicants of the outcome of the application process over different timescales and by different means, for example phone, e-mail, letter. This information should be provided in the details about their requirements. It is best practice not to contact them until after the deadline for the funding organization to inform applicants about the results of the bidding process has passed. Numerous phone calls from worried applicants before this deadline has passed are a source of great irritation as well as a time-waster for the funding organization.

If you are successful you are likely to move into the project planning or implementation stages (see Chapters 3 and 4). Do remember to inform everyone of your success.

Many project applications are unsuccessful and it is worthwhile obtaining feedback from the funding organization. This will help you to learn from the experience and, hopefully, submit a successful funding application next time.

Whether you are successful or not, do remember to thank those people who have contributed to your funding application.

Summary advice on making a funding application

The following advice for applicants making funding applications is provided at the British Library's Concord website (www.bl.uk/concord/) and is based on their experience of the Co-operation and Partnership Programme's calls for proposals. This advice is relevant to all information workers who are making a funding application:

- Read the documentation carefully: if in doubt, ask.
- Pay particular attention to the scope of the funding scheme, to priority areas and to any specific exclusions.
- Take note of the criteria for selection and for assessment and make sure all relevant issues are addressed.
- Provide all the information specified and as clearly as possible: additional information or clarification may not always be sought before the proposal is sent to referees or considered by a Selection Panel.
- Do not assume that referees or Selection Panel members will know the detailed background to your project proposal.
- Demonstrate how your project fits the funding scheme and its priorities.
- Avoid jargon.
- Be realistic about the proposed start date of your project, bearing in mind the published timetable for the funding scheme and, if applicable, the time needed to recruit staff.
- Provide evidence that all partners are committed to the project.

They also provide a list of common comments from referees on unsuccessful project proposals and these include:

- Insufficient detail provided to enable an assessment to be made.
- Insufficient detail about aims/methodology.
- Deliverables not clearly defined.
- Timetable insufficiently detailed/lacking milestones.
- Costs not broken down/justified.
- Awareness of relevant related work not demonstrated.
- Roles and responsibilities of partners unclear.
- Lack of/weak dissemination/evaluation plans.

Managing the finance

Once you have obtained agreement to go ahead with the budget and start the project then you will need to manage the finances and keep appropriate records. This, in theory at least, is no more difficult than managing your personal finances. What it involves is keeping records of all project income and expenditure, and keeping copies of all the paperwork, for example receipts, quotes, invoices. Normally all these records will be kept on the accounting system used by your own organization and it is worthwhile spending time with the accounts staff to make sure that you understand and are using the system correctly.

Once the project starts you will need to monitor the project costs. This is most easily managed using a spreadsheet and updating it regularly. You will need to keep a cumulative report which shows the actual and the planned costs. This will enable you to respond to unexpected changes in expenditure.

Many project managers find that their original budget included as part of the project proposal does not match with the reality of running the project. Estimates of expenditure may differ from the actual expenditure. For example a project manager may have estimated a cost of £2100 on software and £5400 on hardware but then once the project is up and running find that they need to spend £1100 on software, £3500 on hardware and £2000 on specialist furniture (the latter not being included in the original budget). In this situation the project manager can approach the funding organization and ask permission to *vire* or transfer the funding from one budget heading to another. Most funding organizations are used to receiving requests for virement from the grant holder and will readily agree to the change. In this situation it is vital that all the paperwork is retained even if it is only an e-mail confirming approval to vire the funds, as it will be required for audit purposes.

Project managers are normally required to produce summary reports of the project financial information, for example at monthly or three-monthly intervals. This involves updating and then printing off the relevant spreadsheets. Again, your finance department will be able to help you with this. In the early stages of your project it is worthwhile working through these summaries with an experienced member of staff who will explain the layout and meaning of different parts of the report.

Audits

Many funding organizations require, as part of the contract, that the recipients of their funds obtain an auditor's report in order to demonstrate that they have properly accounted for their grant. This means that the project manager or their organization must employ an auditor to audit the project finances. The responsibility of organizing the audit may be managed by the organization's finance department who will already be working with auditors, although in some situations a project manager may be asked to organize the audit themselves. If you find yourself in this situation it is worthwhile taking time to identify a firm or individual who has experience of auditing projects funded by grants. The author is very aware (from a previous painful experience) of the hazards of employing an auditor with minimal experience of auditing externally funded projects: this can lead to a situation where much time is wasted in explaining the project process and funding regime.

Arill and McLaney (2003, p.112) state: 'The main duty of auditors is to make a report as to whether, in their opinion, the financial statements do that which they are supposed to do, namely, show a true and fair view and comply with statutory and accounting standard requirements.' In order for the auditor to carry out an audit they will need access to all the project records (electronic and paper-based) including contracts, payroll details, invoices and receipts. Their job is to ensure that all the finances have been correctly accounted for and that there is a paper trail demonstrating the expenditure of every penny! The easiest way to prepare for an audit is to ensure from the very start of the project that all the correct records are maintained and that a record of every expenditure (backed up by receipts) is maintained. Make sure that you have written confirmation (e-mail or letter) of any changes in budget that you re-negotiate with the funding body.

Summary

This chapter illustrates the importance of external funding for library and information projects. Bidding for funding is an important aspect of project working and finances are available from a wide range of sources. This chapter outlines the bidding process and emphasizes the importance of research and matching the requirements of funding organizations. It includes guidelines for project managers for successful funding applications. Multi-source funding offers special challenges to project managers and team workers. Once project funds are available then they need to be managed in accordance with the project contract and also organizational financial rules and procedures.

References

Arill, P. and McLaney, E. J. (2003) *Accounting: an introduction*, 3rd edn, London, Prentice Hall Europe.

Brewer, S. (2002) *Overview of Funding Streams for Libraries and Learning in England*. Report commissioned by Resource, www.resource.gov.uk/.

Parker, S. et al. (2001) *The Bidding Culture and Local Government: effects on the development of the public libraries, museums and archives*, Resource Report 113, http://online.northumbria.ac.uk/faculties/art/information_studies/imri/rarea/im/pubsec/bidcul/psbidcult.htm.

Pearn, A.. (2002) *Bidding Strategically*. Paper presented at The Bidding Culture: CURL Task Force on Staffing Resources. Conference held at University College London, 13 June 2002, www.curl.ac.uk/about/biddingculture.html.

Thake S. (2001) *Building Communities: changing lives*, York, Joseph Rowntree Trust.

7

Using ICT to support the project

Introduction

The aim of this chapter is to explore the use of information and communications technology (ICT) to support project management. As a result of reading this chapter, readers will have an overview of the diverse range of virtual communication tools and their use in supporting the project management process. In addition the chapter explores the project management software that is often used to plan, monitor and help manage the project information process.

Virtual communications

It is hard to imagine working in the library and information world without access to electronic communication tools such as e-mail and discussion lists. Virtual communication tools are widely used in libraries as a means of communicating with their users, providing an important channel for many information workers to communicate with their colleagues and also network both across the profession and with other professions. In today's fast-paced work environment virtual communication tools are essential for enabling project communication processes to take place in a timely manner. This section is an updated and rewritten version of an earlier work by the author (Allan, 2002).

The types of virtual communication tools most commonly used in projects include e-mail, mailing lists, bulletin boards, webforms, polling, instant messaging, chat or conferencing, internet telephony and videoconferencing. These can be divided into two main types:

- *Asynchronous tools*. These enable project workers to communicate at a time that suits them. Individuals post a message that is held by the system. This message can be read and responded to as and when the recipient comes online. Asynchronous communications take place over time rather than at the same time.
- *Synchronous tools*. These enable people to communicate when they log on to the same system at the same time, i.e. they are immediate and live communications. However, unlike face-to-face communications, a transcript or record of the communication process is available in most systems.

Table 7.1 Characteristics of virtual communication tools (adapted from Allan, 2002)

	Type of communication	Asynchronous/ Synchronous	Project management applications
E-mail	One to one, one to many	Asynchronous	Exchange of information Provision of detailed instructions Discussions about current issues Follow-up meetings Problem solving Giving and receiving feedback Exchange of products, e.g. reports
Mailing lists	One to many	Asynchronous	Exchange of information Problem solving Networking
Bulletin boards	One to many	Asynchronous	Exchange of information Provision of detailed instructions Discussions about current issues Collaborative or project work Follow-up meetings Exchange of documents
Webforms	One to one	Asynchronous	Collection of information Exchange of information
Polling	One to one, one to many	Asynchronous	Collection of information Organization of meeting dates
Instant messaging	One to one, one to many	Synchronous	Exchange of information Provision of detailed instructions Problem solving
Chat or conferencing	One to one, one to many	Synchronous	Exchange of information Provision of detailed instructions Discussions about current issues Collaborative or project work Problem solving Follow-up meetings
Internet telephony	One to one, one to a few	Synchronous	Exchange of information Provision of detailed instructions Discussions about current issues Problem solving Meetings Training events
Videoconferencing	One to one, one to a few	Synchronous	Exchange of information Discussions Problem solving Meetings Training events

E-mail

E-mails are an essential tool for keeping in touch with project team members, funders, stakeholders and others. In large projects it is worthwhile spending a little time thinking about how e-mail will be used as there can be a danger that individuals will suffer from information overload. Some projects manage their virtual communications by using closed mailing lists (see below) or group communication software tools (see below) rather than simple e-mails. In some situations a project may use a number of mailing lists, for example the Subject Portal Project uses two team mailing lists (see Chapter 2 and also Martin, 2003).

Mailing lists

As well as sending e-mails to individuals it is possible to send them to groups using mailing lists, also called discussion lists or listservs. The process is managed by a hosting service that maintains a list of all the different discussion lists and the people who subscribe to them. It is run using a mail server, a piece of software that stores a mailing list of individual e-mail addresses. Two common mail server programs are Listserv and Mailbase. This software will copy your message to all the people on the mailing list.

There are thousands of mailing lists available on the internet, each devoted to a particular topic and aimed at a specific audience. Project managers and team members may want to subscribe to relevant existing mailing lists as a means of keeping up to date on their subject and in some projects they may want to set up their own project closed mailing list.

Joining or leaving a mailing list is a simple matter of sending an e-mail. Information about these lists is available from a number of sources including:

- Topica (www.topica.com/)
- Catalist (www.Isoft.com/catalist.html)
- JISCmaiL (www.jiscmail.ac.uk)
- Liszt.com (www.liszt.com)
- Reference.com (http://reference.com).

In addition to mailing lists being used as a means of communicating within the project they are also an important source of information and advice as they enable library and information workers to keep up to date and network with each other. They offer an important source of professional help and support. One of the advantages of using them is that responses to queries are provided by people working in the field and so they often give up-to-date, down-to-earth and practical advice. However, a word of warning: the information you gain from a mailing list may be inaccurate, out of date or biased. In the author's experience, if this does happen it often results in a fast and furious set of replies from other subscribers who are all too anxious to correct the misinformation. See Table 7.2.

Example   How to install an access control system in less than four months and live to tell the tale

'I was anxious to pursue the replacement card problem. We upload all of our student borrower data from a central university system. When students lose their cards the central system issues a new card with the same student number but it adds a replacement number to the end. We needed to be able to invalidate the old card and activate the new one. . . . I needed someone who really knew their stuff. I explained my predicament on the Talis email list and waited expectantly. Astonishingly quickly I received 2 replies both helpful, one from Warwick and one from Birmingham. Over the next couple of months we received a huge amount of help from Birmingham University, who run the same access control system as Brookes, use Talis and have a very similar replacement card problem.' (Hall, 2002, p.2)

Setting up a mailing list is relatively simple, requiring that you make some basic decisions:

- Is the list open to anyone to join or is it a closed group only open to project workers?
- Do you want the list to be moderated, i.e. messages are vetted before being posted to the list, or unmoderated, i.e. subscribers can post up their own messages?
- Do you want to send digest messages? These collate all the messages received that day and send them out as one e-mail. An index or contents page may be included in the digest.
- How will you manage the mailing list? Mailing lists normally need someone to facilitate the list and ensure that individuals don't dominate the list or introduce their own private agendas, or that personality conflicts don't interfere with the smooth running of the team and the project.

Table 7.2 Making best use of mailing lists (adapted from Allan, 2002)

Dos	Don'ts
Spend some time getting to know the group and its interests before sending your first message.	Use it for personal messages to individuals who subscribe to the discussion list.
Keep to the topic.	Send a message or response if you are feeling angry/upset by something you have just read.
Send clear and concise messages.	Get involved in personal disputes.
Use short quotations from previous messages to keep the context clear.	Use it to advertise.
If you ask for information consider summarizing responses for the whole group.	Forget that it is a team or public forum.
Be polite and consider other people's feelings.	

Discussion or bulletin boards

Bulletin or message boards provide a facility for discussion under various topic headings and not in real time. They allow individuals to respond to topics or threads in the group, or to begin a new topic or thread by posting a comment or question. Any messages sent to a discussion group are permanently visible to everyone who has access to it.

Message boards may be used by a project team and may be located on a project, website or made available via group communication software, such as LotusNotes, or for people working in education environments by using virtual learning environments such as Blackboard or WebCT. Discussion groups are extremely useful to project teams as they enable team members to communicate with each other at a time and place that suits them.

A wide range of software packages enable the use of bulletin boards within websites. Sometimes online registration is required before you can access a bulletin board. A typical bulletin board provides the following features:

- indexes
- basic search facility, e.g. by topic, author, keywords
- tools to enable you to view bulletins in a hierarchical format (this is often called threaded or unthreaded where they are sorted by date/time)
- facilities to enable messages to be selected, saved and downloaded
- facilities to indicate whether or not the user has read a particular message, e.g. red flags for unread messages.

Webforms

A webform is a form or questionnaire that individuals must fill in online either as a means of providing information or requesting information. Webforms are commonly used in library and information units as a way of providing online reference services. They may be used in projects in a number of different ways:

- disseminating and obtaining responses to a questionnaire, e.g. during the project evaluation phase
- obtaining feedback from project workers.

Polling

Polling enables you to quickly set up a survey or questionnaire and obtain feedback from a wide range of people. It has a wide range of uses in project management including:

- obtaining feedback from project workers or other stakeholders
- setting up and running simple questionnaires

- organizing meeting times, e.g. online chat or face-to-face session.

Polling software is available from a number of sources including www.soomerang.com.

Instant messaging

Instant messaging enables you to send and display a message on someone's screen in a matter of seconds. Instant message systems often have friend or buddy lists that watch to see when one of the people on your list comes online so that you know the instant when you can start messaging them. For some people this may sound like a nightmare scenario, but it does offer the opportunity to provide immediate access to help and support. An example of when instant messaging may be used in project management is to provide additional support to staff who are piloting new systems or procedures who may want an instant response from you. Instant messaging obviously depends on both people being online with the relevant instant messaging systems in place.

Examples of instant messaging software include ICQ ('I seek you') available from www.icq.com and AOL Instant Messenger available from www.newaol.com/aim. The key to successful use of instant messaging within the project team is for all parties to have discussed and agreed how it will be used. It is important to set clear boundaries around its use; otherwise it can become a major irritant and distraction.

Chat or conference rooms

Chat or conference software enables users to hold a 'live' discussion by sending each other short written messages. Some chat software only allows one-to-one communications but increasingly chat software enables groups to take part in 'live' discussions. Chat software may be used to support individual team members, provide quick advice and guidance to a member of staff working remotely, or as a coaching tool. If the project involves working in virtual teams then team meetings may be held using online chat or conference sessions (this is explored in more detail in Chapter 8). Group communications software and virtual learning environments normally include chat or conference software that enables these synchronous conversations to take place and they may be supported by tools such as whiteboards.

Chatting online has a number of advantages: it can be a private form of communication, it is immediate and the text can be saved for future reference. Chatting online can be helpful for people with hearing or speaking impairments and it can also ease communication among those for whom English is a second language. In addition the text of chat sessions can be used for training purposes. As with most tools, there are disadvantages and these include the absence of non-verbal signals and the need to learn how to send and be comfortable with short telegraphic messages between two or more people. Some people don't feel comfortable with this form of communication and there is the potential danger that the other person may log-off and 'disappear'. However, an increasing number of people are becoming very experienced with this form of communication and there is an entire internet subculture built around chat.

Tips for using chat or conference rooms

- Appoint a chairperson.
- Signal when you want to speak using a '?'. The chairperson then invites you to speak.
- Send short messages.
- If you want to send long messages split them into chunks and indicate that a message continues either with '(more)' or by using a series of full stops.
- Limit your conference room sessions, e.g. to no more than an hour or one item of business. Most people find chat sessions demand high levels of concentration.

Tips for joining a conference

- When you enter a conference room and other people are already present you will not be able to see the discussions that took place before you arrived.
- Indicate your presence with a 'Hello'.
- Wait a minute or two so that you can understand some of the context of the conversation.
- Once you feel ready then plunge in and get going.

Internet telephony

Synchronous communications now include internet telephony, which is the ability to make phone calls via the internet. The advantage of internet telephony is that it enables individuals to make long-distance phone calls through the computer and the internet without paying expensive long-distance phone charges. However, it requires relatively up-to-date computers with access to a fast modem and large RAM memory; otherwise the sound quality can be poor.

Individuals using the internet for phone calls need to obtain a microphone for the computer and also to install internet telephone software. Increasingly organizations are combining internet telephony, e-mail, traditional phones, voice mail and facsimile transmissions into powerful new unified messaging services.

Videoconferencing

Videoconferencing has been available for years but previously required specialist and very expensive equipment installed in specialist rooms. In recent years videoconferencing packages have been developed for use on standard desktop computers. The use of desktop videoconferencing doesn't appear to be widely spread in ILS but its use is increasing.

Example   Managing a project across a number of cities

The author once worked in a university where the learning resources department was located in three cities in the north of England. She was involved in a project made up of three sub-projects, each located on a different site: the move of an existing learning resource centre to a new building; closure of a campus; and split of the stock from an existing campus to a new building. Each sub-project was led by a team leader and there was also a team leader from the technical services department who managed the computerized information systems which included the catalogue. These staff were distributed across three cities and project team meetings were expensive to hold (because of travel expenses) and also time consuming as individual team members could spend up to three hours travelling between the campuses. As a result a mixture of different types of team meetings were held: face-to-face meetings, videoconference meetings and hands-free conference telephone meetings. The face-to-face meetings were particularly used for thrashing out the overall strategy and handling major problems or issues. Videoconferencing and telephone conferencing were found to be effective for shorter meetings which focused on items that were not controversial. The amount of time and money saved by cutting down on the distance meetings was appreciated by everyone!

Providing integrated virtual communications

Project teams and managers frequently need access to a combination of virtual communication tools and there are three main ways of providing this facility: having a project website, using communications software packages and using a virtual learning environment.

Project website

The use of project websites was considered in Chapter 6 and, if required, they can be developed to include a range of virtual communication tools, for example discussion boards and conferencing facilities. Some projects operate two websites, one for the project team and one for the public, and in this instance the project team website may include a range of communication tools. One example of this approach is found in an e-mentoring project that can be accessed at www.empathy-project.org.uk, and the home page for project members is illustrated in Figure 7.1. These plug-ins can be introduced into the website relatively easily (see Benjes-Small and Just, 2002).

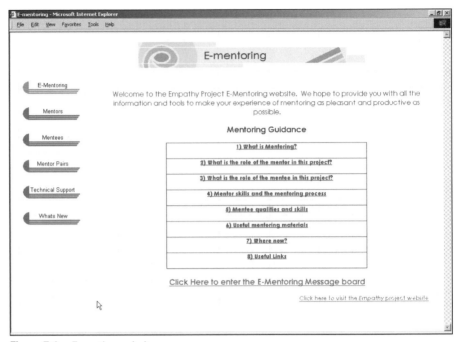

Figure 7.1   Empathy website

Communications software packages

Many organizations now use commercial communications software packages that offer a mix of e-mail, messaging, bulletin board and conference room facilities. Many of these packages also offer:

- a knowledge management facility, e.g. through the use of document file systems with built-in content indexing and a search facility to help users find and share information quickly
- a basic project management system, e.g. task management including scheduling, to do lists and automatic reminders
- data and videoconferencing, including real time conferencing, document authoring, whiteboarding, text discussion and file transfer.

Common examples include LotusNotes and Microsoft Exchange 2000. For project managers working within an organization where staff commonly use these systems it offers the advantage that staff will be familiar with the systems so that their project work and particularly their communications with each other become firmly integrated into their day-to-day activities.

Example   iCohere

iCohere is a groupware collaboration software platform that can be integrated into the parent organization's existing site or used as a standalone collaborative platform. Everything is managed through simple templates using a standard web browser so system administrators do not need specialist technical knowledge to manage the site. It provides project managers with an extensive range of facilities including:

- announcements
- shared documents and extensive document managing system
- real-time instant messaging
- real-time group meetings
- customized databases
- integration of streaming PowerPoint files and other media
- contact information including photographs
- website links
- security features.

iCohere has an extremely user-friendly interface with helpful and unobtrusive use of colour and icons. For example in the discussion board it is possible to mark your personal responses, as shown in the following examples:

- 'Yes, I agree' (accompanied by a thumbs-up sign)
- 'Next steps . . .' (accompanied by some steps)
- 'I have a different perspective' (accompanied by a pair of glasses)
- 'Here's a new twist' (accompanied by a spiral shape with an arrow)
- 'Here's a resource' (accompanied by a book).

For project teams that are considering running a virtual conference this type of software provides a valuable and relatively easy approach to setting up and managing the required conference facilities. During 2003 the author attended a virtual conference that was hosted on the iCohere software and she found that it took a very short amount of time to become familiar with the conference and its layout. In fact it was probably quicker to do this than it would be at a large traditional conference where one has to navigate around a number of different buildings. The virtual conference mirrored a face-to-face one with keynote presentations (based on PowerPoint with audio), follow-up discussions (real-time and through bulletin boards), papers with follow-up discussions, workshops and a series of informal sessions, e.g. in a café. One of the advantages was that the site was kept open for 60 days after the conference so it was possible to revisit presentations, papers and discussions. More information on iCohere is available at www.icohere.com.

Virtual learning environments

Project workers in the education field often have access to virtual learning environments such as Blackboard or WebCT. These may be used as a tool for facilitating project communications as they commonly contain the following facilities:

- e-mail
- announcements
- bulletin board
- chat or conferencing facilities
- facilities for sharing documents and other electronic resources.

A project manager is able to create their own project site and then use it as a focus for virtual communications. The actual process of setting up the site is relatively easy, for example an experienced practitioner would be able to complete a basic site in a couple of hours. However, the process of gaining access to the site may be cumbersome because of the approaches used by colleges or universities to organize and administer their virtual learning environment. This is demonstrated in the following example:

Example   E-learning project

During 2002/3 the author was involved in an e-learning staff development initiative involving three universities in the United Kingdom. The original plan meant that 40+ participants would need access to a virtual learning environment for the length of the project. A review of the learning environments of the universities showed that only one of the universities was able to offer easy access to a wide range of practitioners. The other universities all had their access requirements built around the needs of their student population and dependent on individuals being enrolled on specific modules of study. Although this problem could have been by-passed the project team decided that it would take an immense amount of work and so their preference was to select the university system that gave very easy access to a wide range of participants.

Project management software

The aim of this section is to provide a general guide to project management software by outlining the typical features of these packages, identifying some important sources of information on them and finally evaluating their use by library and information workers.

What is project management software?

Project management software enables you to store the project plan electronically and then edit and update it. Common project management packages such as MS Project will enable you to carry out a number of activities:

- planning the project
- viewing the project and obtaining reports
- tracking progress
- supporting team communications
- managing multiple projects.
- The following section is based, in part, on the work of Carroll (2000).

Planning the project

The main use that library and information workers appear to make of project management software is to plan their project and produce a range of reports. These are then used as a management tool throughout the project without further use of the project management software. The typical functions that are available include the abilities to:

- input information about the project tasks, duration, links with other tasks and resources
- produce a calendar that shows working days, holidays, weekends
- produce GANTT charts (see Figure 7.2)
- produce PERT diagrams (see Figure 7.3) and automatically identify the critical path

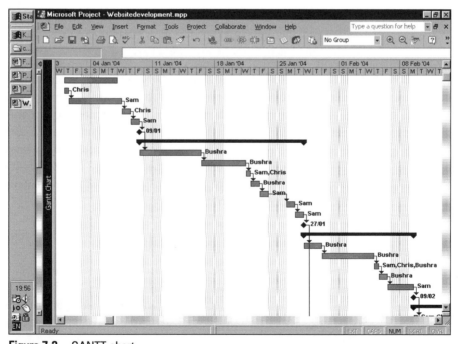

Figure 7.2   GANTT chart

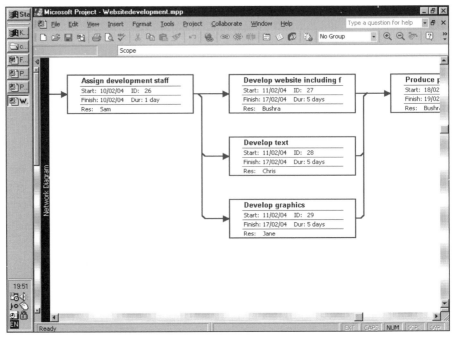

Figure 7.3   PERT diagram

- produce detailed information about resources, e.g. allocating people to tasks, scheduling people; they also help with resource levelling, i.e. identifying people who are over- or under-scheduled and then either manually or automatically levelling or smoothing out the allocation of people to tasks over time.
- manage the project costs by creating a basic budget.

Project management software is particularly useful at the planning stage as it can be used to identify potential conflicts or constraints in the project plan. The risk analysis (see Chapter 2) may be used to generate a series of questions that test the robustness of the plan and whether or not it includes sufficient time and resources for contingencies. In particular these packages enable you to forecast and ask 'what if?' questions such as 'What will happen if the data input takes 25 days instead of the estimated 15 days?' or 'What will happen if it takes twice as long as predicted to produce the website?'

Viewing the project and obtaining reports

The software will typically hold vast amounts of data or information and you can then select how you view this (on a computer screen) and/or obtain reports or printouts that focus on either task information or resource information. The basic views include GANTT chart, PERT diagram, resource sheet, resource usage and calendar.

The software will typically enable you to produce a range of reports or printouts, which may include overview, current activities, costs, assignments (who is assigned to which task), workloads (e.g. workload per person per week or month) and customized reports, for example a to do list for each individual team member, list of critical tasks, etc. (see Figure 7.4). Many packages include filter functions which allow you to select specific individual or groups of tasks and also individuals or groups of people. These reports may be copied into other packages, for example Word or Excel, which means that it is relatively easy to produce a written project plan that integrates this information.

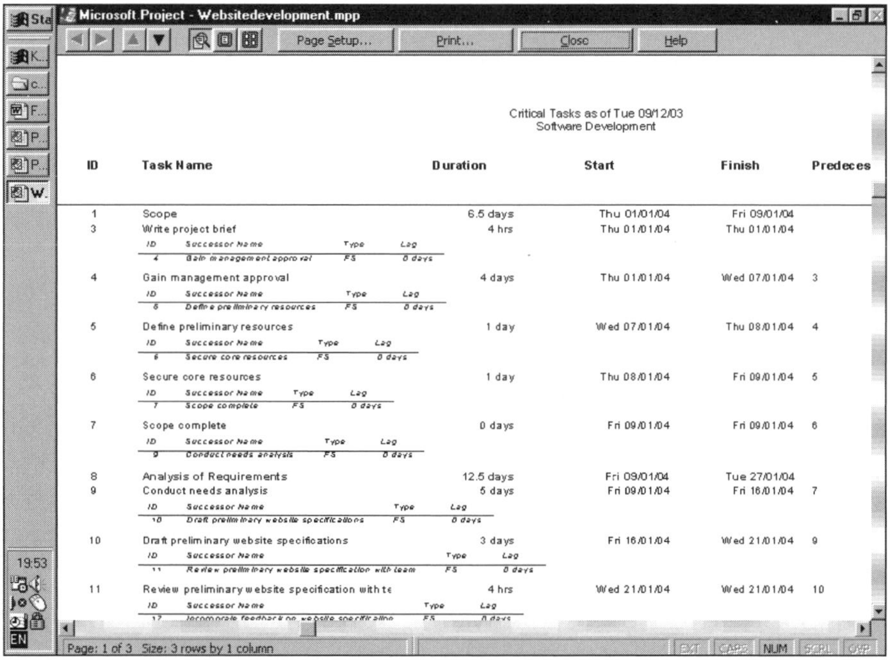

Figure 7.4 List of critical tasks

Tracking progress

Once the project starts to be implemented you can track its progress with the help of project management software. In this situation the original plan is often called the *baseline plan* and this is permanently saved or set. As the project progresses information (about tasks, resources and costs) is added to an *actual plan*, which is an updated version of the baseline plan. The information that is added to the actual plan will include completed tasks or part-completed tasks. Information may be added to the actual plan as and when it suits the project team, which, in reality, will tend to be on a daily or weekly basis. As you enter the data the software will recalculate and reschedule the project and this new *schedule plan* contains the tasks that have not yet started or those that are part completed.

During the tracking progress stage of a project it is possible to obtain different views or printouts of the project including completed work, part-completed work, percentage completed, actual vs baseline, tracking GANTT (showing the actual state of the project compared with its baseline) and project statistics. These may be copied into Word or Excel files and presented as part of a project progress report.

Supporting team communications

Some project management software packages, for example MS Project 2000, provide add-ons such as Project Central that will support team communications. Project Central supports collaborative working between a project manager, team members and senior managers. It includes the following types of facilities:

- Auto accept features may be used to designate the information that may be directly added to the system and also that which needs to go through a review process before it is added.
- Individual team members may input project progress information directly into the software.
- Project managers may request status information from individual members, which is then integrated into one report.
- Team members may view a day-by-day work plan and their own customized GANTT chart.
- Team members may input information about the actual hours that they work on the project and also information about their availability, e.g. as a result of holidays.
- Team members may (with permission) delegate tasks to others in the team.
- Senior managers may access project summaries and, if they require, the details of the project and its progress.

Managing multiple projects

Nowadays many project managers and team workers are involved in working on a number of projects at the same time. This can be a complex process as there needs to be an overview of the projects as a whole so that the people working on them are allocated across all the projects and their workload levelled out. This is illustrated in Figure 7.5 where the shading indicates the portfolio of work of one team member. At the same time if changes occur, for example the time taken to complete a task on one project overruns, then the resource implications for the other projects need to be identified and managed.

Project management software such as MS Project will help the project manager work with more than one project at a time by consolidating the projects, i.e. it groups them together and creates a consolidated project file. In the same way the human resources are managed and co-ordinated through a resource pool. If there are inter-project dependencies it is possible to set them up in the same way as it is for one project (see Chapter 3).

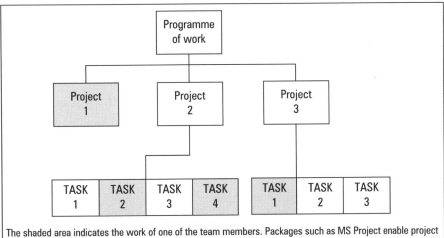

The shaded area indicates the work of one of the team members. Packages such as MS Project enable project managers to allocate this work and then manage it by identifying resource allocation and any work over-allocated. The software will enable the project manager and team members to obtain views and printouts identifying the individual's tasks and their workload, e.g. as a weekly 'to do' list.

Figure 7.5 Managing multiple projects

Project management software packages

There are hundreds of different types of software packages that have been produced to support project managers and workers. Two examples commonly used by the information profession are MS Project and PRINCE2.

MS Project

This Microsoft product is widely used and an evaluation copy may be obtained from the Microsoft website at www.microsoft.com. There is an official MS Project website at www.mpug.org/, which gives access to a wide range of information and useful tips. The examples given in the previous section all relate to MS Project. Freund (2002) summarized its advantages and disadvantages as shown in Table 7.3:

Table 7.3 Advantages and disadvantages of MS Project

Advantages	Disadvantages
Straightforward set-up	Installs some unwanted utilities
Familiar interface	Relatively expensive
Integrates with MS Office	Uses system resources heavily
Excellent tutorials and wizards	Too complex for small projects
Good selection of project management features	
Good collaborative features	

PRINCE2

PRINCE was originally established in 1989 by the UK government's Central Computer and Telecommunications Agency, now called the Office of Government Commerce (OGC). PRINCE was originally developed as a project management process tool for IT projects and PRINCE2 provides project management tools for all types of projects. PRINCE2 may be used with the associated software tools or with a paper-based system. PRINCE2 identifies the following key processes in a project:

- starting up a project (a pre-project process)
- initiating a project
- managing stage boundaries
- controlling a stage
- managing product delivery
- closing a project.

PRINCE and PRINCE2 are owned by the OGC, whose official website is www.ogc.gov.uk/prince/index.htm. There is a Prince User Group and their site is www.pug.mcmail.com/.

Making a choice

One of the problems for project managers is choosing which package to use as they range from basic to extremely sophisticated packages and from free shareware to specialist systems that cost hundreds or thousands of pounds, euros or dollars. Some useful sources of information and critical reviews on project management software include:

- the online *Project Management* magazine, with access to an extensive range of excellent reviews (www.projectmagazine.com/)
- ZDNet UK (http://reviews.zdnet.co.uk/software/productivity)
- Directory of Web-Based-Business Software (www.web-based-software.com/project/)
- David W. Farthing's Software Project Management website (www.comp.glam.ac.uk/pages/staff/dwfarthi/projman.htm).

Do information and library workers use project management software?

An important question to consider at the stage of getting started on a new project is whether or not to use project management software. Chapter 3 considers the project-planning process and outlines how project plans may be put together using paper and pen or by using project management software. Alan Boughey (2000) carried out a small survey in a UK public library discussion group on the use of project management software. He quotes one favourable response: 'I personally found it very useful for setting out tasks, milestones, responsibilities, relationships between tasks, and connections between them etc.' His survey also indicated that these public librarians considered that project management software worked best for complex projects that were carried out over a long period of time.

Boughey also found that the positive responses emphasized that they were only using very basic parts of the software and quotes 'I was able to show a colleague the basics in 15 minutes.' Feedback also identified that even the enthusiasts said that MS Project appeared to be very complicated and that experience of other MS Office products did not seem to help when it came to learning how to use MS Project (this is in contrast to the findings of Freund (2002) reported above). The survey identified that the use of project management software 'was not worth the effort for smaller projects'. Boughey's conclusions are that the use of project management software is 'Marginally favourable. Some libraries are using project management software, but it looks as if you need a fairly high degree of IT literacy and it has to be a long-running, more complicated project to make it worthwhile.'

Informal discussions with information workers who have used MS Project has produced the summary in Table 7.4 of the advantages and disadvantages of using software such as MS Project in a library and information context.

Table 7.4 Advantages and disadvantages of using project management software

Advantages	Disadvantages
Most packages are relatively easy top use	Relatively expensive
Impact of changes can be identified easily	Time required to learn software package
Provide a range of views/reports of the project	Data input can be time consuming
Reports can be incorporated into project documentation	Garbage in/Garbage out (GIGO)
Useful for managing large or complex projects	Too complex for small projects
Different team workers can access the project management information	People treated as 'resources' in software and project managers and team workers need to remember that they are individuals
Provides a professional image	Provides a means of managing information; it is *not* the project!

Summary

This chapter has outlined two different types of ICT that may be used to support project managers in their work. Virtual communications such as e-mail, discussion lists and online conferencing may be used by teams that work together in a face-to-face situation as well as by entirely virtual teams. The use of virtual communication tools needs to be considered at the analysis and planning stages in the project and, for large and complex projects, it is worthwhile spending time planning how to use these tools. If this planning process doesn't take place the use of virtual communication tools may lead to information overload. Project teams frequently need access to a combination of virtual communication tools and there are three main ways of providing this facility: project website, use of communications software packages or use of a virtual learning environment.

Project management software such as MS Project may be used to store the project plan electronically and then monitor and control the project. It enables the project manager to focus on very detailed information, for example who is doing which task on which date, and it also provides an overview of the total project process. One of the main advantages of using project management software is that it can be used to generate a wide range of printouts for use by the project manager and team. In the library and information world project management software appears to be used at the planning stage of relatively simple projects, which are then managed using paper-based methods, and for both planning and managing complex projects.

References

Allan, B. (2002) *E-learning and Teaching in Information and Library Services*, London, Facet Publishing.

Benjes-Small, C. M. and Just, M. L. (2002) *The Library and Information Professional's Guide to Plug-ins and Other Web Browser Tools*, London, Facet Publishing.

Boughey, A. (2000) *Project Management Software – Summary of Responses*. Source: lis-pub-libs, http://bubl.ac.uk/news/surveys/su032802.htm.

Carroll, J. (2000) *Project 2000 in Easysteps*, Southam, Computer Step.

Freund, J. (2002) Microsoft Project Standard 2002, http://reviews.zdnet.co.uk/software/productivity.

Hall, F. (2002) How to Install an Access Control System in less than 4 Months and Live to Tell the Tale, *SCONUL Newsletter*, **25**, (Spring), 87–9, www.sconul.ac.uk.

Martin, R. (2003) Turning Gateways into Portals, *Library & Information Update*, **2** (6), 52–3.

Part 3
Projects and people

8

The people side of projects

Introduction

The purpose of this chapter is to explore the people side of projects. Nowadays library and information workers may find themselves working in a variety of team situations ranging from small in-house teams through to multi-skilled teams and collaborative teams made up of workers from a variety of professions and organizations. The latter type of team is particularly found in partnership working and is considered in more detail in Chapter 9.

This chapter explores the people side of projects from the project manager's or co-ordinator's perspective. It starts by considering the fundamental requirements for project workers such as the need for a good-quality working environment and basic human resource management practices. The chapter then considers strategies for managing the team, including the characteristics of effective teams, getting started, life of teams, team roles, effective team working, challenging situations and reviewing team work. This is followed by a section that explores working across different cultures, for example with people from other countries or cultures, from different organizations or generations. Increasingly library and information workers are involved in working in virtual teams and the realities of virtual team work are explored and guidance given for project managers. Finally, the chapter explores the project manager's role in managing the people side of change that arises from the project.

Fundamental requirements for project workers

Chapter 2 outlines the different types of information workers (contract and permanent staff) who may be involved in working on the project. Many projects employ short-term contract staff and it is vitally important to ensure that they have access to a range of essential working requirements and services. These include:

- appropriate working environment, e.g. desk, computer with internet connection, telephone
- relevant organizational information, i.e. information about the employing organization, the ILS, the project
- copies of organizational policies, e.g. equal opportunities policy, bullying and harassment policy, use of ICT and e-mail policy

- personnel information, e.g. contract, details about policies and procedures relating to holidays, sick leave, pensions.

New contract staff will need to be provided with an induction process, access to a performance management or appraisal process, staff development, mentoring (if the ILS operates a mentoring scheme) and also career development support at the end of their time with the project. Research described in Chapter 10 suggests that contract staff often miss out on some of these essential processes, as shown in the following example.

Example   An isolated project worker

The author worked for a very short time on a university-based retrospective catalogue conversion project. At the start of her contract the induction process took about 15 minutes and she discovered that her 'office' was a desk in the corner of a book store. She met her line manager once a month and these meetings were completely focused on the tasks in hand and whether or not targets had been met. At no time was there any discussion about her experiences on the project. There was no discussion about her staff development needs or her career after the project. As a result the author left this project as quickly as possible and moved on to another role. The project manager then had to find and train another project worker who also left the project after a very short time . . .

It is assumed that permanent staff have access to an appropriate working environment and also all of these human resource management systems and processes. Informal discussions with project workers indicate that they often find it difficult to focus on their project work when they are at their desk as they are interrupted by their everyday work, routine phone calls and requests for help. In this type of situation it is often useful to have a project office where the project workers can come and focus on their project work and not be torn between the demands of their everyday and project work.

Managing the team

Effective teams are those where individual members come together and work in such a way that individuals' knowledge, skills and experience complement each other and individual and team performance is enhanced.

Larson and Lafasto (1989) studied a wide range of teams including a Mt Everest Expedition Team and the Boeing 747 team and they identified the characteristics of high-performing teams team as follows:

- a clear, elevating goal
- results-driven structure

- competent team members
- unified commitment
- collaborative climate
- standards of excellence
- external support and recognition
- principled leadership.

The development of a high-performing team involves a range of activities which perhaps starts with the project manager reflecting on the team and its needs. There are many different teams involved in ILS projects; the author has experienced the following types:

- in-house team in an academic information service which was made up of people who were really keen to become involved in the project and also people who were 'conscripts', i.e. they had been asked to be involved and were perhaps quite negative about the project, working with you, working in a team, or other aspects of their work
- in-house team in a college library where the project manager had no line management responsibilities for team members
- in-house team where one of the team members was a senior member of staff from another department
- in-house team in a voluntary organization made up of paid workers and a couple of volunteers
- cross-sector project team where all team members were employed by different local organizations and members ranged from very senior to very junior staff
- national project team involving like-minded information workers who were all at a similar stage in their careers
- project team made up of library, information technology, administrative, academic and educational development workers in a traditional university.

Each of these different types of teams are likely to require some time in coming together and working out how to work together. The project manager needs to consider their style of management and how they will lead the project team. In general a collaborative and facilitative management style is likely to work well with team members and it will enable individuals to feel ownership for the project. The following sections consider different aspects of the team development process; this is explored with respect to working in partnership in Chapter 9.

Getting started

The initial team meeting is extremely important as it sets the tone for the whole project. It is really important that this meeting is organized in such a way that team members feel welcomed and that the whole project experience is going to be a positive one. Factors that can help oil the process include clear instructions about the meeting and travel arrangements, and also refreshments on arrival. The agenda of this meeting (as stated in Chapter 3) is likely to include the following:

- introductions
- the project brief
- areas of concern: hopes, fears and expectations
- project aims, outcomes and milestones
- project management and governance
- project team: roles and responsibilities
- project processes: ground rules and working practices
- other questions and answers
- outline action plan.

This initial meeting is all about getting to know each other and the proposed project. The project brief provides a useful starting point to ensuring that everyone understands the project and its boundaries. The meeting is also about identifying and agreeing working practices. A useful way of establishing team member and project manager responsibilities is to ask the meeting to split into sub-groups and for each group to identify the responsibilities of team members and the project manager. These can then be shared and written up on a flipchart. The final list can then be used as an informal contract for the project team. The project manager may find it useful to keep this flipchart paper; then if people don't fulfil their responsibilities this activity can be revisited. When the author carried out this activity at the start of a project the suggestions listed in Table 8.1 were made.

Table 8.1 Team member and project manager responsibilities

Team member responsibilities	Project manager responsibilities
To attend project meetings	To organize, monitor and control project
To agree realistic targets/deadlines	To keep the costs, meetings and administration to a minimum
To complete project tasks as agreed in meetings	To ensure that information about the project is communicated to the stakeholders
To inform team of current or potential problems	To keep the team informed of all developments
To provide or suggest potential solutions to problems	To give positive feedback and to support the team
To support team members and the project manager	To keep the project in line with ILS and organization's policies and procedures
To manage their own time – for both the project and routine ILS activities	To make sure the project complies with legal requirements
Not to whinge or whine	To provide tea and biscuits at project team meetings

It is worthwhile using some time at the first meeting to let people air any concerns, fears or unhappiness about the project. One way of managing this process is to ask the team to work in smaller groups, for example groups of three or four, and to identify their 'hopes and fears' for their involvement in the project. They can then feed back to the whole group. In the feedback process it is important to ask for the 'fears' first as this will raise any negative issues. Once these have been dealt with then move on to the 'hopes'. Managing the process in this way will mean that you end up on a positive note. If necessary set a time limit on the feedback process or limit each group to two fears and two hopes. This helps to prevent the whole process being swamped by potential negativity. At this stage it is worth mentioning that the majority of project teams are made up of positive and constructive staff!

Managing a project team involves focusing on and working with individuals, the team and the task. As project manager you will need to know the individual team members and their strengths and weaknesses. You will be involved in action planning, giving and receiving information and feedback from team members, e.g. through e-mails or phone calls, and providing them with help and support as required. An important aspect of team work is motivation and you may be required to spend some time motivating and supporting staff.

Life of teams

Some knowledge of team work is valuable for project managers and common ideas about team development and team roles are useful as they provide potential tools for managing the team process. It is common knowledge that teams go through a development cycle that is made up of five stages:

- forming
- storming
- norming
- performing
- adjourning.

At each of these stages a team is likely to go through a set of experiences and if, as project manager, you are aware of these stages it means that you are less likely to be surprised by what happens with the team and also that you can use some standard intervention techniques to help the team progress. It is worth noting that teams may spend different amounts of time within each stage and also that they may get stuck in a particular one. If your team does appear to be stuck within one of these stages then Table 8.2 provides some ideas of ways to move the team forward.

Table 8.2 Stages in team development

Stage	Characteristics	Facilitation techniques
Forming	Individuals are starting to get to know each other. Some people may be shy and quiet. Others may be over-participative. People may 'cling on to' people they already know. There may be confusion about the purpose of the project and how it will work.	Give people time to get to know each other. Encourage and enable people to talk to those people they don't yet know. Make sure that the initial meeting covers the topics outlined earlier in this chapter. Follow up absent members and ensure that they have a full briefing.
Storming	Individuals may challenge the project leader or other team members. They may also challenge the concept of the project and its processes. There may be personality clashes and differences of opinions about how to carry out the work.	Provide time for people to 'let off steam'. Ensure that the intended project working practices are fully discussed and agreed by everyone. Be clear about what is and what isn't negotiable. If there are some people in the team who appear to be very disruptive then see them by themselves and sort out their issues. Occasionally you may need to make a decision about whether or not you keep someone in the team or ask them to leave.
Norming	In this stage, people begin to settle down and get on with the task. The unwritten rules or 'norms' of the group develop. The team establishes set ways or 'norms' of carrying out its work. Everyone knows what to expect and how events such as meetings will be run.	Highlight and clarify working practices. Agree standards of work. Ensure that the norms that are set are useful ones, e.g. that everyone arrives on time for meetings. Provide time in meetings to discuss working practices and their effectiveness.
Performing	There is a high level of trust within the group. Individuals accept each other and their strengths and weaknesses. There is a strong commitment to achieving the group goals and people work flexibly to achieve them. This stage is often accompanied by increased use of humour , 'in-jokes' or stories.	At this stage the project manager takes a relatively low profile. The team is working well. Your role is to support and facilitate the team. You may be asked to intervene with respect to specific problems.
Adjourning	The project is coming to an end and the team is about to disband. This stage is characterized by 'good-bye' rituals – celebratory party, exchange of personal information and ideas for meeting up in the future, exchange of stories about the project and what they have achieved.	Organize some kind of closing event. This may range from special cakes at a meeting through to a party. Give time at the final meeting to evaluate the project and the team's achievements. Make sure that you thank everyone for their work on the project.

Example

A project was established to improve the signing and guiding in a multi-site academic learning resource centre. The project leader (Jane) called a series of team meetings with team members drawn from each of the college sites. At the first three meetings each learning resource centre sent a different representative and the project leader felt that all the time was being spent on introductions and explaining the project rather than moving on to carrying out the work. She identified that the group hadn't formed because of its changing membership. She also decided that the best person to sort out the problem was the director of learning resources (Emily) and she arranged to see her. As a result of this meeting Emily sent out a message to each of the learning resource managers saying that they needed to select a representative who would be able to attend every meeting. This intervention meant that the project team was able to form and the project then got going.

Team roles

Another important aspect of project work relates to the team roles that individuals take on as a result of their personality rather than their formal role within their organization or the team. Probably the most common approach to team roles is that described by Meredith Belbin (1981) who identified the roles listed in Table 8.3.

According to Belbin each of us has our own team role preference(s) and these are the areas in team work that we find the easiest to contribute to. However, it's worth pointing out that, as with most models, this is an over-simplification and as individuals who behave in sophisticated ways we can move into team roles other than our preferred role. This model can be used by a project manager in a number

Table 8.3 Belbin's team roles

Team role	Characteristics
Co-ordinator	The co-ordinator will clarify goals and facilitate decision making and group working. The co-ordinator will co-ordinate the tasks and activities and also chair meetings.
Team worker	The team worker has good people skills and will promote harmonious working relationships. The team worker is good at listening and averting friction between people.
Resource investigator	The resource investigator is likely to be an extrovert, enthusiastic and a good communicator. The resource investigator is very good at identifying opportunities and is likely to have a wide network of contacts.
Shaper	The shaper is challenging, dynamic and works well under pressure. The type of person who is able to 'move mountains' and may be impatient with others.
Monitor evaluator	The monitor evaluator is a thinker who looks at all the options and evaluates a situation before making decisions. The monitor evaluator is unlikely to be carried away by emotion as they will focus on facts.
Implementer	The implementer turns ideas into action. The implementer is down to earth, conscientious and reliable.
Plant	The plant is creative and very good at coming up with potential solutions to problems. The plant may be unorthodox.
Completer finisher	The completer finisher is conscientious, follows up the detail and makes sure that tasks are finished and delivered on time.
Specialist	The specialist provides unique and specialist knowledge and related skills. The specialist is single minded and dedicated to their own area of work.

of different ways. For example, questionnaires are available via the internet (e.g. www.belbin.com/belbin-testing-options.html) that enable individuals to identify their preferred team roles. This could be used as a group activity at the forming stage of a project team. The ensuing discussion about individuals' strengths and allowable weaknesses can help the team to pull together during the life of the project.

The model can also be used informally, for example when reflecting on a project team meeting, to identify individuals and their preferred roles. The findings can then be used to help construct an action plan for managing the team, for example if the team doesn't have a natural completer finisher then it may be useful to allocate this role to one or more people.

Example

A project team was established within a government library with the function of developing an online tutorial for information searching. After three meetings of this team there appeared to be very little productive work taking place. Team members were enthusiastic and kept arriving at meetings with new ideas and information about research on online learning and tutorials. One person carried out very detailed though rather specialist research on new and upcoming technical tools. However they hadn't carried out the agreed actions from the previous meeting. The project co-ordinator identified that the team contained people whose preferred roles were plants, shapers or specialists but lacked team workers, completer finishers and implementers. As a result, he decided to expand the team to include people whose preferences would complement the existing team strengths. In the new team and as a way of getting the team to re-form he introduced a team activity based on the Belbin model. In addition, the co-ordinator identified the importance of managing the balance between completing the work and keeping the team interested and enthusiastic about the project. As a result of these actions the project team was able to move forward and complete their remit.

Effective team working

All project workers, whether working on contracts or carrying out project work as part of their 'normal' ILS role, need to be able to work as effective team members. Informal discussions with participants on project management workshops identify the following qualities of effective project team members. They:

- are punctual
- communicate clearly and honestly
- communicate regularly, e.g. by e-mail
- exchange information
- are flexible
- contribute their share of the workload
- identify problems (and come up with potential solutions)

- give and ask for help
- give constructive feedback
- keep their promises
- meet deadlines.

The main barriers to effective project team work were apparently caused by individuals who:

- talked down the project
- were cynical about the project and its potential value
- whinged or whined about the project, project manager or project team
- 'disappeared', e.g. went on holiday without informing the project manager or other colleagues
- didn't respond to e-mails or phone messages
- didn't keep their promises and deliver their work on time
- kept vital information private to themselves
- weren't prepared to be flexible and help other team members who were perhaps struggling
- moaned about their workload
- arranged to be away from work during critical times of the project.

Managing challenging situations

In any project that involves different people working together there are likely to be some disagreements and conflict. Common problems that arise in project and team work include individuals not pulling their weight, someone not sharing information, disagreement about a particular decision, wasting time, too much work, confusion and/or personality clashes. The ability to reach agreement and resolve conflict is an important part of effective team working. It is important to deal effectively with any problems that arise during your work as a team as the consequences may be that you fail to meet your goal. This could lead to repercussions such as: the ILS losing a client, a contract, money and its reputation; the team losing credibility, power or team members or being disbanded; and/or individuals being blamed, achieving poor appraisal results or even losing their jobs.

Conflict and disagreements need to be tackled and there are a number of different ways in which this is commonly done at work:

- *competition*, which involves the creation of win/lose situations; this is likely to result in the 'losers' feeling aggrieved and possibly loosing their motivation for the project.
- *avoidance*, where the conflict is ignored in the hope that it will go away
- *compromise*, where the individuals concerned each find a way of giving up something while gaining part of what they require

- *consensus*, where discussions take place until everyone agrees on a particular course of action
- *collaboration*, where a solution is found that satisfies everyone's requirements
- *accommodation*, where one or more people will put the needs of another above their own needs.

Competition and avoidance are not particularly effective ways of dealing with conflict or disagreement. Ideally, the project co-ordinator and team needs to find a way of compromising, reaching consensus, collaboration or accommodation over the issue. There are many different approaches to proactively managing conflict; one useful strategy is the 'Five-step plan':

1 Identify the source of conflict.
2 Understand each person's position.
3 Define the problem.
4 Search for and evaluate alternative solutions.
5 Agree upon and implement the best solution.

The first step is to analyse the situation and identify the source of conflict. This may be an obvious source or it may be an indirect one. The next step is to give everyone a chance to have their say. Let them report the facts of the situation. They will also need to share their feelings. Listen to what they have to say. Remember to read their body language too. Using the information you have gained from the second step define the problem. Summarize the situation as you see it. Check that everyone agrees with your definition. As a team, look for alternative solutions. You may want to ask for assistance, for example from an expert. Once you have obtained a number of potential solutions then evaluate them, e.g. by listing their advantages and disadvantages. As a team, agree the best solution. Make sure that everyone agrees positively and that their verbal and non-verbal language are congruent. If anyone looks unhappy with the solution then discuss it with them. Once everyone is in total agreement, implement the best solution.

Reviewing team work

When and how do you review team work? The process of identifying and spending some time reviewing team work is likely to be repaid as the team learns to become reflective and learn from their successes and weaknesses. Team work may be reviewed regularly, for example every month or every three months, and be dealt with during regular team meetings. The following questions may be used as prompts for reviewing team work:

- Did you achieve your objectives?
- Did you produce work to the required standards?
- What were your main successes/failures?
- In what areas did you not achieve your objectives?

- Did working as a team help or hinder the achievement of your objectives?
- Did you produce better or worse work as a result of working in the team?
- How effective was the team in working together?
- Did the team help and support individuals in their work?
- What were the main strengths and/or weaknesses of team work?
- How could you improve your outcomes?
- How could you improve team working?
- What are the main learning points for next time?

Working across different cultures, countries and organizations

Project work, as with much information and library work, frequently involves working together with people from a range of cultures: different organizational cultures, different countries and perhaps generations. Culture is extremely deep-rooted and includes unconscious values, for example about ways of behaving with other people, different practices with regard to such matters as rituals, heroes and symbols, and different ways of being. Hofstede (1994) identifies six layers of culture: country level (where we live or have lived), regional and/or ethnic and/or religious and/or linguistic affiliation level, gender level, generation level, e.g. teenagers, young professionals, over 70s, social-class level associated with educational opportunities, occupation or profession, and finally organizational or corporate level (for those who are employed).

Hofstede also identifies four cultural dimensions that project managers need to take into account when they are working across national boundaries:

- *Individualism*, i.e. the extent to which people think of themselves as individuals or members of a group. In individualistic countries such as France, Germany or Canada people are expected to look after themselves and important values to them are personal time, freedom and challenge. This is in contrast to collectivist cultures such as Japan, Korea or Greece where individuals are bonded through strong relationship ties based on loyalty, e.g. to the family, team or employer, and the team or group is considered more important than the individual.
- *Power distance*. This is concerned with the distance between managers and workers and the importance of hierarchy. In high-power-distance countries such as Latin America and many Asian and African countries, workers tend to be afraid of their managers and leaders (who tend to be paternalistic and autocratic) and treat them with respect. In contrast in low-power-distance countries (such as the USA, the UK and most of Europe) workers are more likely to challenge their managers who will tend to use a consultative management style.
- *Gender*. In countries such as the USA, Japan, Hong Kong and the UK, where the masculine index is high, people tend to value challenging work, opportunities for gaining a high income, personal recognition for their work, and opportunities for advancement to a higher-level job. In countries such as Sweden, France, Israel

and Denmark, where feminine values are more important, people tend to value good working relationships, co-operative behaviours and long-term job security.
- *Certainty dimension.* This relates to the extent to which people prefer unstructured and unpredictable environments as opposed to structured and predictable ones. Cultures with a strong uncertainty dimension such as South Korea and Japan will tend to avoid unknown situations which they will perceive as threatening. In contrast in countries such as the UK, USA, Netherlands, Singapore and Hong Kong where uncertainty avoidance is weak, people feel less threatened by unknown situations. They are also more likely to be open to innovations, risk, etc.
- *Time orientation.* Countries such as China, Hong Kong, Japan and Taiwan demonstrate a long-term time orientation which is characterized by persistence, perseverance, a respect for a hierarchy of the status of relationships, thrift and a sense of shame. In contrast countries such as the UK, Canada, Germany and Australia have a short-term orientation and this is marked by a sense of security and stability, a protection of one's reputation, a respect for tradition and a reciprocation of favours.

The implications of this model for any project manager or information worker is to be aware that if your team is made up of people from different countries then they are likely to have different approaches to their work. Individuals who are experienced in working within a collectivist culture are likely to find that they are on familiar territory with collaborative team work but they may feel exposed if asked to work in an extremely individualistic manner. In contrast a team that is predominately made up of information workers from countries with a low-power distance may inadvertently exclude a team worker from a high-power-distance country who is not familiar with or comfortable with the rest of their team's relationship with their manager which includes challenge. At the same time, a project manager may enjoy working with uncertainty and ambiguity during the project process and may find it frustrating that other workers, for example from cultures with a strong uncertainty dimension, want high levels of structure imposed on the project.

Hofstede's work is useful as it reminds us that different people have different needs and will work and relate to each other in very different ways. The danger with this type of categorization is that it will be used to stereotype and label people, so it is important to remember that individuals within a culture are extremely diverse too. The key message for project managers is to get to know their team and the individuals within it. You will then be able to adapt your management style to take into account the different needs of individual team workers.

Hofstede also identifies the importance of organizational culture, which he distinguishes from national culture. Organizational culture relates to a whole series of dimensions including:

- process oriented vs results oriented
- employee oriented vs job oriented

- parochial vs professional
- open system vs closed system
- loose control vs tight control
- normative vs pragmatic.

Different library and information services and their parent institutions will demonstrate different organizational cultures by being located in different positions on these dimensions. This is particularly relevant to project managers and teams who are working in partnership on collaborative or co-operative projects. This issue is followed up in more detail in Chapter 9.

Virtual teams

Increasingly library and information workers are involved in projects that involve working across national boundaries and time zones. In these situations much of the project communication processes may take place using e-mail, videophones, telephones and teleconferencing in addition to the possibility of online discussion groups and chat or conferencing. Some project teams never meet face to face while others may meet once or twice during the life of the project.

One common strategy for circumventing geographic and time constraints is to work in virtual teams using online communication tools such as e-mail, discussion or bulletin boards and conference or chat rooms. These tools are explored in Chapter 7. While working in virtual teams gives individual members the opportunity to access the project communication processes from their desktop at a time and place that suits them it also raises some challenges to team work. How do you develop trust and confidence in the team and its members if you have never met them? How do you manage a project team whom you have never met? How do you take into account the different cultural backgrounds of information workers from a wide range of countries?

Working together in face-to-face teams gives individuals the opportunity to size each other up, get to know each other's work style, habits and preferences and build relationships. In particular sitting around a meeting table means that you gain very quick feedback from someone's replies (or their silences) and also their body language. In contrast virtual team working involves communicating with other team members through text (in the case of e-mail, discussion groups or conference rooms), sometimes with the support of video-streamed images, e.g. in the case of videoconferencing. Yet individuals need to get to know each other and develop their trust in their project manager and team members

The five-step model based on the work of Gilly Salmon (1999) and adapted in Table 8.4 for reference to virtual team work provides a helpful outline of the key stages in virtual team work.

Table 8.4 Five-step model of virtual team work

Stage	Team member activities	Project manager activities
Stage 1 Access and motivation	Setting up system and accessing	Welcome and encouragement Guidance on where to find technical support
Stage 2 Online socialization	Sending and receiving messages Getting to know each other Starting to develop a team culture	Introductions Ice-breakers Ground rules Netiquette
Stage 3 Information exchange	Exploring roles, responsibilities, project tasks Carrying out activities Reporting and discussing findings	Facilitating structured activities Assigning roles and responsibilities Encouraging discussions Summarizing findings and/or outcomes
Stage 4 Project work	Completing project tasks Giving and receiving feedback Problem solving	Facilitating online activities Monitoring process with respect to project plan Facilitating the process Asking questions Encouraging reflection
Stage 5 Closure	Completing all project tasks Completing review and evaluation processes Goodbyes	Leading review and evaluation process Ensuring loose ends are completed Leading closure

Adapted from the Five-Step Model of Salmon (2000)

In virtual teams the role of the project manager includes managing technical, project and social aspects of the communications process.

- Technical
    - ensuring an appropriate virtual communication platform
    - ensuring appropriate technical support
    - ensuring that the administrative arrangements e.g. user IDs and passwords are in place
- Project work
    - overall management of project work
    - monitoring and controlling tasks and activities
    - provision of feedback and support to individuals and group(s)
    - offering advice and support with respect to problems
- Social aspects
    - development of an appropriate online working environment
    - development of friendly informal communications.

Here are some examples of the types of activities that online project managers are likely to be involved in in order to encourage an effective virtual project team:

- Stage 1   Access and motivation
  - Ensure that the online team is set up with a welcome message.
  - Ensure team members know how to access the online group.
  - Open and close the discussion group.
- Stage 2   Online socialization
  - Lead a round of introductions with, perhaps, an online ice-breaker.
  - Welcome new team members or late arrivals.
  - Provide a structure for getting started, e.g. agreement of group rules, Netiquette.
  - If individuals break the agreed group Netiquette tackle them (either privately or through the discussion group).
  - Wherever possible avoid playing 'ping pong' with individual team members and ask other people for their opinions and ideas.
  - Encourage quieter team members to join in.
  - Provide summaries of online discussions. This is called weaving and involves summarizing and synthesizing the content of multiple responses in a virtual group.
- Stage 3   Information exchange
  - Provide highly structured activities at the start of the group life.
  - Encourage participation.
  - Ask questions.
  - Encourage team members to post short messages.
  - Allocate online roles to individual members, e.g. to provide a summary of a particular thread of discussion.
  - Close threads as and when appropriate.
  - Encourage the online group to develop its own life and history. Welcome shared language, metaphors, rituals and jokes.
- Stage 4   Project work
  - Facilitate online activities.
  - Monitor process with respect to project plan.
  - Facilitate the process.
  - Ask questions.
  - Encourage reflection.
- Stage 5   Closure
  - Ensure 'loose ends' are completed.
  - Highlight team achievements.
  - Encourage (structured) reflection and evaluation on team process.
  - Thank team members for their contributions and work.
  - Formally close the project.

Some of the challenges of working in virtual teams

Working on this type of project can be particularly challenging, as demonstrated in the examples below.

Example   Working across two continents

Paul is a UK citizen currently working on an international food project in the USA. He is based in New York and regularly contacts project members in Chicago (one hour behind New York time). Sometimes he needs to pick up issues raised in discussions with Chicago-based team members, explore them with individuals located in France (six hours ahead of New York time) and then discuss them with people in the UK (five hours ahead of New York time). At times he feels as if his working day is never ending as he must communicate 'live' with team members across the world using virtual conference rooms and conference calls, and sometimes this involves getting up early and working during the evening. In his office he has a series of clocks, one for each team member. This helps him to make contact at the right time of day.

Example   Working in a government library and information service

Jane is the senior librarian in a UK government library service that has libraries in more than 20 locations around the world. She is currently leading a project that involves working with six librarians (on full- and part-time contracts) who are located in different countries within the European Union. Jane says, 'There are no real problems about communicating with the dispersed team: as with ILS staff in the UK I chiefly use e-mail and then telephone. The only problem that arises is that with some countries I have only a two-hour block (11 a.m.–1 p.m.) when we are all at work. If I forget to phone them during this time, and pressure of work means that this sometimes happens, then I have 'lost' another day on the project. This can be very frustrating. It just means that I have to be very well organized all the time.'

Practical experiences for ensuring effective virtual team working

Below, a number of information workers who are involved in virtual team work present their practical tips for effective online project work:

> My recommendations include making sure that individuals post their biography with a photograph. This is very helpful at the starting phases of a project. In our team we also posted up our particular strengths and experiences (those relevant to the project) and also things that we really disliked! This helped us to get going.   (Jane, e-learning officer, UK college)

As part of our introductions we identified national holidays. The project involved us in working across four different European countries and being aware of different people's holiday periods made it easier when we came to working out the project schedule. (Jose, information worker, Netherlands)

Our project involved librarians working in three different time zones (UK, USA – Pacific Time, and Australia). We organized our conference sessions at different times. This meant that we shared amongst us the 'pain' of having to get up early or stay up extremely late to be able to talk with each other. It seemed to work well. I found it quite exciting being online to colleagues in different countries at times I wouldn't normally be working.

(Sam, information worker, pharmaceutical industry)

I recommend holding face-to-face meetings whenever possible and, particularly, at the start of a project. They just speed up the whole team process and it is so much easier when you actually meet people and can start to get to know them. Although it can be expensive if people have to travel long distances it helps the team to gel and the whole project to start on a sound basis.

(Don, academic librarian, USA)

Buy a series of clocks and put them on your wall. Set them to the times of the different countries where your team members are located. Attach their names to labels and put these beside the clocks.

(Paul, information worker, food industry)

Managing the people side of change

Projects result in change. Projects that are focused at an operational level, for example introduction of a new service or the design of a new website, may result in relatively small changes. In contrast major projects, i.e. those that have an impact at a strategic level such as re-structuring an ILS or merging an information and ICT service, are likely to result in major changes. As a result the project manager will need to consider how to manage the change and its impact on people. When you are introducing major changes into the ILS you are likely to be subject to pressures that will make this change process difficult. A major cause of resistance to change is the responses of individuals to the change process.

The actual response to the project and its resultant changes will depend on a variety of factors. Some changes may be viewed as positive, such as moving to a new building with fabulous resources, or negative, such as the merging of two units or departments. The same change may be viewed differently by different team members, for example the introduction of a new online reference service may be welcomed by some staff while others may see it as a bad move and one that will interfere with their relationships with the reader. Some changes will be major, e.g.

the restructuring of an ILS with job losses, or relatively minor, e.g. changing over to a new IT system. In essence the more staff have invested in the old situation and the less they are committed to the new one then the greater their psychological responses to the change. This means that the management of change becomes even more important in these situations.

Many people feel apprehensive about going through change and they may go through a psychological process that is similar to that experienced in bereavement. Individual responses to change typically involve a number of distinct phases:

- Phase 1: Shock
- Phase 2: Defensive retreat
- Phase 3: Acknowledgement
- Phase 4: Adaptation and change.

The shock phase may be signalled by staff feeling overwhelmed by the news and responding with panic and feelings of helplessness and numbness. This phase may last minutes, hours, days or weeks. This is then often followed by what is called a defensive retreat where staff may attempt to maintain old structures and avoid their new reality. This stage is sometimes accompanied by feelings of indifference, euphoria or anger. Again, this stage may last from minutes to weeks. The next stage is the one where staff begin to acknowledge the situation and begin to face reality. This stage may be accompanied by feelings of indifference or bitterness. The final stage is one of adaptation and change and here staff begin to build their lives and gradually regain their confidence and self-esteem in the new situation.

It is worthwhile remembering that individuals are likely to move through these phases in their own time and this means that within any single team there may be individuals at each of the different phases. In addition, some staff may still be engaged or 'stuck' in this cycle as a result of previous changes within the ILS and, in this situation, as project manager you will be managing the current responses to change as well as responses to previous changes.

The different strategies required for managing and supporting people through change are summarized in Figure 8.1. As a project manager an awareness of these responses to change is important as at different stages you will need to focus on different aspects of the change process. For example when staff are experiencing shock it is important to focus on the communication processes and to provide lots of opportunity to explain the current situation. You will need to remember that they may not remember everything that has been communicated to them and so you are likely to need to repeat the message, perhaps many times, and give lots of reassurance.

In some situations the project manager may be working through this psychological process themselves, for example they may be asked to manage a project such as the closure of a library with very little notice. This may mean that the project manager is experiencing shock at the same time as their colleagues. This is an extremely challenging situation to be in as the project manager must provide leadership and guidance at a time when they are personally experiencing a variety of emotions. In this situation it is vital that the project manager has support and guidance, perhaps from a mentor, and this is explored in Chapter 10.

Be adaptable Delegate Monitor Support Mentor Encourage flexibility of approach Value considered risk taking	Provide a vision for the future Explain and keep on explaining Talk to individuals Communicate, communicate, communicate Listen, listen, listen Give reassurance Put the change into perspective Do not give out too much information – keep it simple Handle people with great sensitivity Keep your feet on the ground Be available
Phase 4 **Adjustment**	**Phase 1** **Shock**
Phase 3 **Acknowledgement**	**Phase 2** **Defensive retreat**
Provide more detailed information Keep listening Evaluate options Support realistic ideas and strategies You don't have to provide *all* the answers Provide direction not control Involve as many people as possible in the planning process Acknowledge positively people's efforts	Don't panic! Don't take staff reactions personally Keep listening Allow people to let off steam Highlight the positives Keep meetings to the point Don't get hooked into win/lose situation Use a wide range of strategies

Figure 8.1 Managing and supporting people through change (original source unknown)

Summary

Project management involves working with different groups of people and an essential part of the project process is building and developing constructive relationships with both individuals and teams. A knowledge of the life cycle of a team and team roles can be used by project managers and teams to support the project process and as a basis for developing a positive team culture and effective working practices. Many project teams are made up of people from different cultures, countries and organizations so an awareness of these issues and the needs of individual project workers is essential for successful project work. Guidelines are provided for working in virtual teams. Finally, project work often results in change and the project manager will need to manage the impact.

References

Belbin, R. M. (1981) *Management Teams – Why They Succeed or Fail*, Oxford, Butterworth Heinemann.

Hofstede, G. (1994) *Cultures and Organizations*, London, HarperCollins.

Larson, C. E. and Lafasto, F. M. J. (1989) *Teamwork: what must go right, what can go wrong*, Newberry Park, CA, Sage.

Salmon, G. (2000) *E-moderating*, London, Kogan Page.

9

Working in partnership

Partnership is one of the most complex and difficult ways in which to work. When it works even reasonably well, however, it can bring some of the best results for the end-user.   (Daker, 2003, p.47)

Introduction

Library and information workers have always had a tradition of networking and collaborative working, both within the profession and also with other professional groups. In the last decade governments, agencies and organizations have raised the profile of partnership working as they see this as one way of meeting the needs to modernize and develop new approaches to working and delivering services in a complex and rapidly changing environment. A scan of the current ILS literature reveals that many information workers are now involved in developing and delivering a wide range of services through partnerships.

This chapter will explore the realities of working in partnership and it will focus on five themes: the context for working in partnership, benefits of working in partnership, challenges of working in partnership, processes of working in partnership, and managing the partnership.

Context for working in partnership

Sullivan and Skelcher (2002) highlight the rise in collaborative working between the public, private, voluntary and community sectors, and they map out how collaboration is central to the way in which public policy is made, managed and delivered in the UK. Partnership working is currently popular with the UK government where it is seen as an important strategy for tackling complex and interlinked problems such as crime, education, health and housing in our inner cities. Partnership working is one way in which the modernization agenda is being tackled. It involves collaboration with partnerships in health and social care, social inclusion, and education which includes a lifelong learning agenda involving many public and other library and information services. Financial drivers are often used to ensure that the different sectors and agencies work together in partnership to deliver services and products.

A wide range of partnerships exist and these may be located within a region or country, transnational, e.g. European, or global. Pilling and Kenna (2002) provide an excellent overview of collaborative initiatives in the information world, which covers the UK national and regional perspectives, co-operation in specific fields (higher education, preservation), European and international co-operation, and funding. The following examples show the range and scope of some projects.

Example   Libraries and sport

Manchester Libraries children's services worked in collaboration with top ice hockey and basketball teams to encourage children to read. A wide variety of activities took place including a special televised home match on Family Reading Night involving cheaper entry on the production of a library card and attendance at the match by well known children's authors who gave away copies of their books. Moody writes: 'The fantastic response from children, schools and community groups has shown us that the support from both teams is more than just a good way of promoting reading. It's also given us great confidence to know that we can establish successful high profile partnerships and deliver good quality, ambitious projects' (Moody, 2000, p.2).

Example   The YouthBoox project

Partnership working frequently involves information and library workers collaborating with other professionals, as demonstrated in the YouthBoox project in Shropshire which involves a youth librarian, youth workers and a professional story-teller working together. It is funded by the Arts Council of England's New Audiences scheme and is an action research programme, exploring which reading 'hooks' work most powerfully with teenagers. See www.literacytrust.org.uk/Pubs/robhunter.html.

Example   AIM25

AIM25 is a project funded by the RSLP (Research Support Libraries Programme) and its aim is to provide a web-accessible database of descriptions of the archives and manuscript collections of colleges and universities in London and the surrounding area bounded by the M25 London orbital motorway. This includes some of the royal colleges and societies of medicine and science based in London. More information is available on the AIM25 website at www.aim25.c.uk.

Example   European Union

The European Union has supported an extensive range of regional collaborative initiatives. One significant example is the Telematics for Libraries programme that supported 87 main projects and involved more than 350 parties, of whom half were libraries. The Telematics projects produced a variety of outputs and notable examples which have had a significant impact on the library and information community include the standards such as UNIMARC and EDIFACT and also freeware tools. See www.cordis.lu/libraries/.

Example	International co-operation

The London School of Economics in the UK and Macquarie University in Australia are involved in a co-operative project to provide a 24 hour IT help desk. Further information is available from www.lse.ac.uk/itservices/help/Helpdesk/rehds.htm.

Benefits of working in partnership

What are the benefits of working in partnership? Informal discussions with some directors of library and information services and also with project managers produced the following list of benefits of this type of work:

- Enhanced access to people, resources and organizations.
- Enhanced ownership – projects that are set up to collaboratively tackle specific problems are owned by the partners and this means that the project outcomes are more likely to be accepted and owned by the partner organizations.
- Enhanced quality – the involvement of a wide range of people who bring their different professional perspectives can enhance the quality of the project experience and outcomes. Individual partners may be more willing to take on new ideas and working practices as a result of the partnership.
- Increased exposure to new ideas/approaches – working in multi-professional teams can help partners to broaden their outlook and obtain a broader understanding of their work and their context.
- Improved use of resources – partnership working not only enhances access to resources but also leads to more efficient use of resources.
- Enhanced motivation – being part of a successful partnership can boost morale and help individuals to develop new enthusiasms for their work. However the opposite may be true too!
- Continuous professional development – working on a collaborative project provides individual workers with the opportunity to develop their knowledge and skills.

Partnership working does bring learning opportunities for the different partners, which can be the result of 'enforced' reflection on our own perspectives and working practices in comparison with those of our partners. This is illustrated in the following example.

Example   Lessons from working in partnership

'The partnership effort for the LOGIC grant was also a learning experience for us. Some of the things that we discovered include:

1   Local public libraries are interested in partnering with the University library, particularly if the topic is one of sustaining interest to the involved libraries and the community.
2   While it is important for all libraries to work together, it is also necessary for one of the libraries to take the lead in submitting the grant proposal and to track the financial information.
3   There also needs to be a day-to-day coordinator for the project who is a member of the steering committee, acts as liaison between the consultant and the Steering Committee, establishes meeting times and agendas, and assures that the required reports are submitted on time.
4   Regular meetings of those involved in the project are important not only for progress reports but to maintain momentum and interest in the project.
5   If possible, tasks should be allocated to the various members of the group as a means of maintaining interest and promoting active involvement in the project.
6   Partners take a more active role when they have a strong interest in the project or when the project is tied to their daily responsibilities.
7   The larger and more diverse the partnership group, the greater is the need for communication and coordination.
8   Partnership activities always take longer than anticipated and they require more work and attention than planned.
9   The possibility for partnerships is unlimited. Opportunities arise when least expected and being alert for these possibilities enhances the potential for finding partners for your project.
10   Projects of interest or benefit to the local community have the highest potential of attracting corporate partners as well as community interest and partners' (Horn and Leung, 1999, pp.4–5).

Challenges of working in partnership

Despite the benefits, there are some challenges to working in and leading collaborative teams or partnerships. These challenges may be the result of:

- long-held rivalries or competition
- different values and beliefs
- power struggles
- differing perceptions/perspectives
- potential commitment of large amounts of time, resources and energy

- differences in systems and procedures
- differences in organizational cultures
- responses of people or organizations *not* involved in the partnership.

Example   SureStart

In the UK the development of a wide range of government initiatives, e.g. Education Action Zones, SureStart and Connexions, has resulted in some information workers being involved in innovative project work in collaboration with other professional workers. These initiatives sometimes lead to the development of new forms of work organizations where a project leader with responsibility for a project is working with individuals who may or may not be employed by the project and may be line managed by other staff, e.g. public library managers, though they are physically located and work within the project. This type of project work can be extremely rewarding and also very stressful. Discussions with a number of library and information workers involved in a SureStart project in a Northern City in the UK identified a number of challenges.

The SureStart project was made up of staff from different agencies such as health, social services, lifelong learning (including public libraries) as well as voluntary sector organizations. The line managers of these staff were not the SureStart project manager who was often involved in lengthy negotiations with agencies concerning working practices. Even the simplest situation, for example what happened on the morning of the Queen Mother's funeral, was made complex because the staff working on the project were all on different types of contractual arrangements. In reality this meant that their working practices on such an occasion varied so that some staff were given the morning off work and others an hour off work, while others had no time off for this national event. The project manager had little say in what could happen on that morning as the staff she 'managed' were all line managed by different managers working in different agencies, each with its own custom and practices.

Another example that demonstrates the complexity of working on the project was the matter of identity. 'Who are we and who is our employer?' is an apparently deceptively simple question. However project workers may have their own employer, e.g. the local authority, and then be seconded to the project for 12 months. Other project workers may be employed by the project while others may have their salaries paid by other agencies and be entirely based within the project. Issues such as name badges raised fierce discussion as some workers wanted to wear their employer's badges, others the project badge and some wore both badges. The project managers explored issues of identity – their own and that of the project – and then used these discussions as the basis for discussions within their own team. Over a year the issue of identity became less important as the project and its staff had developed their own identity.

Example   Challenges of working in collaboration with others in a digitization project

'Some digitisation projects will be undertaken as collaborative ventures between two or more institutions. This can be particularly difficult in terms of management and quality. Each institution (or project site) will need to be subject to a project plan under the management of one person who has overall responsibility for the project (the project director). It may be appropriate for each project site to have a project manager who is responsible for overseeing the project director's instructions. Running a digitisation project across many sites brings up complex issues of quality, i.e. making sure that all sites meet the quality standards that are set at the planning stage. This is further compounded if the different sites are using different equipment to produce the digital images or digitising different types of media. Ideally, a quality assessor should be employed by the lead site to act as independent quality control on all images supplied by the different project institutions. Standards must be set, tested across all sites and a schedule established to test the outputs from the different project partners. For digitisation projects across institutions, a contract must be established to stipulate agreements on methods, quality and timing. Communication can be a particular problem between project sites. Regular visits and meetings should be scheduled to discuss and report on the progress of the project.' (National Preservation Office, 2001, p.21)

Processes of working in partnership

Sullivan and Skelcher (2002) identify and explore different ways of conceptualizing the processes of working in partnership, for example as a life cycle, as a social process. Their life cycle for partnerships is based on the development of collaboration as a series of consecutive stages:

1 *Pre-conception.* The potential partners, agencies and individuals become aware of the possibility of working in partnership and the potential benefits and needs to do so.
2 *Initiation.* Individuals come together and explore the potential of working together in partnership.
3 *Formalization.* The partnership is formalized by implementing an appropriate governance structure and/or committing to a project bid.
4 *Operation.* The project is put into action and partners work together to achieve the project goals.
5 *Termination.* The project closes or transforms itself into another venture.

This model provides a useful template for exploring and facilitating collaborative arrangements and its structure is similar to that of the stages of team development (see Chapter 8). As with the team development model, it is perhaps an over-simplification. Some potential partnerships will not move beyond the pre-conception stage and may stall at initiation. Others may transform into a new venture during the formalization stage when individuals develop a better understanding of their context and the project potential. However, overall this model does help to provide project managers with guidance on how to facilitate a project that involves working in partnership and this concept is explored later in this chapter.

The following two case studies help to illustrate these theoretical views about working in partnership. Both highlight the importance of spending time at the start of a project on the creation of constructive relationships and partnerships. The first case study involves academic library and museum collaborative projects and the second public and scientific libraries in Denmark. In the latter project it is interesting to note that the author of the case study identified the importance of project workers developing a project identity as discussed in the SureStart project example earlier in this chapter.

CASE STUDY Analysis: a look at success and risk factors across four academic library and museum collaborative projects

Nancy Allen and Liz Bishoff (2002) have researched a series of collaborative projects involving libraries and museums and they identify the following success and risk factors as follows:

'**Success factors** include:
- Communication: Communication throughout a project is critical and should include all levels of the organization. Projects should take advantage of both face to face meetings, as well as technology supported communication, particularly email and listservs. Face to face meetings are particularly important at the beginning of a project. Project participants must be able to express needs in the area of communication, so that patterns of communication can change throughout the project . . .
- Policy and Operational Issues: Early discussions of the issues that might lead to conflict among types of institutions is desirable. Most important is to gain an understanding of institutional mission, values, and priorities. Beyond these policy issues, there is a range of operational issues including the impact of web-based collections on gate revenue, security and watermarking, the priority placed on education and outreach programs for specific user categories, metadata standards from the archival, museum, and library communities; scanning standards for different kinds of images, legal issues handled differently by libraries and museums, and issues resulting from the need to select material to be digitized . . . the larger the number of partners, the greater the need to cover these issues upfront.
- Organizational culture: Knowledge of the working methods of the partners, including previous experience in working together is critical. Advanced knowledge of these cultural differences is rare, and generally happens

when there have been prior partnerships. New partnerships need to be aware of the potential for conflict and raise the matter at the earliest point possible.
- Commitment: Commitment by senior management from the outset of the project is critical. . . . Changes in senior management may affect the ability to complete the project as defined.
- Technology: While technology based projects have a built-in level of complexity, it is important that the partners develop a clear understanding on the technology infrastructure needs and how the project will be adjusted based on technology changes.
- Conflict resolution: The project should develop a method for resolving conflicts if and when they arise, usually by using some part of the project management structure.
- Incentives: . . . we think incentives for participation are more closely associated with the values, goals, and mission of the project. Pride in holdings, and the fervent desire to share excellent collections is often the greatest incentive, and mini-grants, equipment or other funding are only enabling tools.
- Advisory Committee: An advisory or consultative structure is recommended enabling the project partners to gain independent assessment and additional expertise when needed. This is important when there is a gap between the expertise of some partners compared to others. Trust is enhanced when there is confidence all around in the ability of all partners to contribute effectively.

Risk factors include:
- Knowledge-base: It is important to understand the knowledge level of the partners on all aspects of the project. This might be in the area of metadata, or scanning, legal issues or contract development. Failure to develop common levels of understanding may lead to a lack of involvement, buy-in on later aspects of the project, or in the long run lead to a delayed or failed project.
- Project complexity: Failure to consider the complexity of digitization projects in general, or a lack of information on specific aspects of project management can cause delays in the project and friction among project partners. In the technology areas of the project, this is most critical particularly when only one partner is responsible for the technology support of the project, and other partners become frustrated with delays or confused by the options and issues.
- Internal project resistance: When there is internal objection to some aspect of the project, delays may occur that frequently are resolved only at the level of senior management.

- Organizational culture: One of the most frequent conflicts arose from the differences in the library community's culture of collaboration and the museum community's culture of independence. Both partners need to see benefit to the collaboration to overcome this issue.
- Differences between the library community's values on access to and ownership of collections, and those issues in the museum community, where there may be concerns about the impact on the museum of a website containing components of the museum holdings in digital form. . . While libraries typically list and describe everything they hold, museums do not. While libraries typically promote collections via their websites, museums often promote only current exhibitions with minimal image material on their websites.
- Interpretation vs. identification: One of the major areas of conflict is in how libraries and museums disseminate information on their collections. Museums will present their collections with value added interpretative information, while libraries generally identify the item and allow the user to interpret.'   (Allen and Bishoff, 2001, pp.8–9)

CASE STUDY Co-operation in public and scientific libraries in Denmark: Net Librarian project

Vera Daugaard (2003) describes a co-operative project which brought together Danish public and scientific librarians and now involves more than 150 of them. The aim of the project was to use the internet to provide easier access to the scientific libraries' knowledge and resources for the general public and the amateur researcher. Daugaard writes

'The advantages of establishing a co-operation were obvious for both parties and consequently – in August 2002 – a joint project between the public libraries and four scientific libraries was launched as a pilot with a view to developing a model for the future co-operation. Denmark's Electronic Research Library (DEF) provided funding for the establishment and the pilot ran until the end of the year 2002.

In order to establish a common service in such a brief space of time, it was essential to create a sound collaboration between the libraries involved, both at management level and among the 'practising' librarians. It was also essential that the 'working Net Librarian' should be able to function normally during the building of the joint service. Accordingly, a steering group was set up to ensure various organizational requirements were met, including one management representative from each of the participating scientific libraries, one representative from DEF, two representatives from Net Librarian and two project co-ordinators (one from each sector). The steering group appointed a project group consisting of a member from each of the scientific libraries, as well as the two project co-ordinators to deal with the practical work in the libraries. If time had not been of essence we probably would have formed a project group with several public librarians. Because of the time pressure the project manager from the "working Net Librarian" was charged with the task of representing the experiences and ideas of the public libraries derived from working with Net Librarian since October 1999. Finally, a software group was appointed to examine the market and try to find a new common software for future co-operation.'

Daugaard (2003, p.2) identifies some key factors for project leaders as follows:

'When setting out on a co-operative effort such as this involving several libraries with different 'cultures' and at the same time having to make our co-operation work across the two library sectors, it is important to allow time for discussing the problems and possible solutions thoroughly. It is no good having too many preconceived ideas, and it is important to listen to each other's points of view in order to find solutions that everyone will be able to live up to. Quality rather than quantity is the operative word. As mentioned above time was also of the essence, so we made a kick start with a working seminar – for members of the project group – running over two days, during which the members of the group got to know each other and were able to concentrate on the various problems which had to be faced. Prior to this seminar the project group was presented to some potential barriers to our ultimate success formulated by the project manager from the public libraries.'

These barriers were technical, practical and mental.

Technical barriers
- Firewalls – the use of different firewalls by the collaborating libraries caused technical problems.
- Simple hardware – staff needed support in using a range of technical equipment.

Practical barriers
- There was a lack of non-written communications in the enquiry process.
- The enquiry form – readers did not want to complete a long form and answer too many 'personal questions'.
- Providing written answers was time consuming for librarians.

Mental barriers
- There were different corporate cultures in the 34 co-operating libraries.
- Lack of privacy – individual communications with readers were now open to all librarians to read and staff were not used to being 'looked at in that way'.

- Local pride and competition between libraries – there was a desire to 'show off' your professional skills.
- There was a lack of knowledge in the individual reader who may not be from your local community.
- Fear of losing local resources – some librarians were afraid that management would cut local resources if Net Librarian was successful.
- Using Net Librarian prevented readers from developing their own information skills and so was in conflict with current library practices of providing user education and then expecting the reader to carry out the searches themselves.
- Reduction in people visiting the library. Some librarians believed that the patrons should visit the physical library and so they supplied answers that directed people to visit the library and borrow books.
- Lack of ownership to Net Librarian – it took time for librarians to feel that Net Librarian was part of 'their' library.

The project group used a range of initiatives to overcome these barriers including seminars, a manual and a mailing list:

Seminars
The libraries that were originally involved in Net Librarian took part in a two-day seminar that 'allowed participants to: give a short presentation of the cultural particularities of own library and town and experience some co-operative exercises to grow trust and build a good group dynamic; discuss mutual expectations for the project. This seminar created a sound basis for the co-operation.'

At the end of the pilot project another seminar was held and this was attended by the steering committee. The focus of this seminar was to establish a common framework and set of protocols for answering queries on Net Librarian.

Start-up seminars are held each time Net Librarian expands and these run for two days and include: a short presentation of the cultural particularities of own town, library and stock of materials; a presentation and discussion of the framework and protocols for Net Librarian; presentation of experiences from existing members; hands-on experience.

Manual
This covers the common framework, procedures for working in Net Librarian including procedures for starting/ending shifts, use of chat software, copyright, confidentiality, frequently asked questions.

Mailing list
The 150-plus librarians involved in Net Librarian all have access to a mailing list where they can participate in discussions about working in Net Librarian.

The Net Librarian service has required libraries to work together co-operatively and develop an independent organization (Net Librarian) with its own culture, ways of working, colleagues, rosters, agreements on co-operation, etc. Daugaard (2003, p.7) writes:

> 'As a Net Librarian it is important to see oneself as part of a national service. We should not consider ourselves as an employee of Herning County Library or the Aalborg University Library when we are manning the service, but as soon as the duty period is finished we must be prepared to change identity and realise that we are back again as a member of staff in our local library. The co-operation is founded on openness as work is done via the web where all the participants may look over anyone else's shoulder. Librarians will feel pressure to do their very best when working in an open environment. We believe that the rewards offered in this unique working environment to share and learn from one another ultimately increase the competencies of every librarian.'

Overall the project has been successful (Daugaard, 2003, p.8):

> 'Despite some difficulties arising in this co-operation process, they are greatly outweighed by the advantages. Both parties had some preconceived ideas about each other and each other's institutions. But these myths have slowly, but surely been demolished over the past 9 months, and through our common project we have gained insight into each other's ways of working, built up a well-functioning network and learned to respect each other's qualities and competencies. We are in no doubt whatsoever that through this common inquiry service we are able to exploit the resources far better, both in terms of materials and competencies – to the benefit and joy of the Danish citizens. Net Librarian is open 84 hours a week and no single library could possibly provide this service. The long opening hours are only possible because we are many who pull together and in this way provide the users with the opportunity of "visiting the library" when otherwise it would be closed.'

The project team hope that they will be able to expand the project and create a national service across the two library sectors.

Managing the partnership

The literature on partnership and collaborative working provide a set of characteristics that distinguish effective partnerships from those that are not effective and, perhaps, fail. Effective partnerships tend to demonstrate the following characteristics:

- There is a clear project goal and objectives.
- The project goal and objectives are shared by all partners.
- All partners have made a commitment to the project.
- There is trust and respect among different partners.
- The project process is transparent and agreed by all the partners.
- The project action plan is realistic and takes into account the needs of the partners.
- Partners share the workload and give each other support.
- There is clear and open communication between partners.
- Partners give and take constructive feedback.
- There is a clear framework of responsibility and accountability.
- Partners invest time into the partnership and their relationships with each other.

This set of characteristics provides a project manager with a 'to do' list for managing the partnership and also the project. The following list identifies some of the characteristics of partnerships that fail:

- *Domination of the partnership by one member or organization*. If one dominant partner takes over this can lead to resentment by other members. It may lead to individual project members not feeling part of the team and withdrawing from the project.
- *Cynical members*. Some partners may be cynical about the project, its funding or working in partnership. This may have a negative effect on the project and team working, and result in a self-fulfilling prophecy.
- *Rotating members*. It is a problem if one or more partners are represented at meetings by different members of staff throughout the life of the project because it means that the project team rarely gets beyond the forming stage and there has to be a constant repetition of previous discussions in order to enable the new members to catch up.
- *Previous history*. Sometimes the past history of the relationships between partner organizations or individuals can have a detrimental effect on the whole partnership. This is particularly true if members use the current project to sort out old scores and battles.
- *Unequal distribution or work or project responsibilities*. If a small number of people take on the majority of the work this can lead to them feeling resentful that they are 'carrying' other team members. It can also mean that other team members begin to lose ownership for the project.
- *Added bureaucracy*. Working in partnership can add another level of bureaucracy to the project work. Partnership working tends to involve more meetings and careful documentation of events. This can often take up more time and resources than necessary.
- *Different cultures*. A potential problem area is the different cultures and working patterns of project partners. This issue is discussed in Chapter 8. Unless these are respected then unnecessary conflict may develop in the project.

- *Inexperienced project manager.* The appointment of a project manager with little experience of working on projects, working across sectors or working in an intensely political context can sometimes lead to the demise of a project.
- *Political interference.* Political interference into the project, e.g. by senior managers, directors and elected members, can lead to problems for the project manager and team.

The initial stages of a partnership are probably the most crucial ones in terms of creating a strong foundation for effective working. The more partners and more complex the project then the greater amount of time and attention to detail needs to be paid to the initial stages. Daker (2003, p.47) identifies the length of the lead time in setting up and running projects: 'organisations considering this complex level of collaboration should allow significantly more lead time for projects with fewer partners. No doubt we will produce the results to time, but all be somewhat greyer for it.'

As with any project team (see Chapters 3 and 8), the first few meetings of partners may involve the following processes:

- introductions
- surfacing expectations, hopes and fears
- creating the vision
- building the objectives
- agreeing the action plan.

The process of surfacing expectations is a simple and yet very important one. Asking partners what they expect as part of being on the project team will enable similar and also different expectations to be aired and discussed. It will also help to prevent theoretically small issues becoming inhibitors to the project process.

Example   Collaborative lifelong learning project

The author was involved in a collaborative lifelong learning project which involved staff from six different organizations and a number of different professional groups: library and information workers, community development workers, teachers, IT technicians and administrators. During the surfacing of expectations activity it became very clear that different people had very different expectations as to the length and timing of meetings that they would be involved in. In part these differences related to the working practices of their parent organizations. For some team members it was very important to end meetings by 5 p.m. at the very latest while other people anticipated (and were quite happy about the idea) that meetings would run through until 6 or 7 p.m. After some discussion the group agreed that all meetings would end by 5 p.m. at the very latest. This discussion and decision helped to prevent conflict at a later stage in the project process.

Once a project is established it is vitally important that all partners are kept on board and engage with the project. This is one of the key roles of the project manager who must create and maintain a 'glue' that holds the project together. This glue may be either informal or formal processes which can be divided into 'soft' or people-centred approaches and 'hard' or procedural and documented approaches. These are outlined in Table 9.1.

Table 9.1 Types of project glue

Soft	Hard
• shared goals(s)	• contracts
• shared values and beliefs	• terms of reference
• common concerns and deeper convictions	• project programs (e.g. Microsoft Project), use
• meetings and social networking	of project management tools such as GANTT
• informal communications, e.g. e-mail or	charts
phone calls	• reporting regimes, e.g. reporting back to senior
• informal feedback	managers
• good will	• funding regimes
• people – such as project managers and	• legal requirements
project team members	

Both types of project glue are important. Effective project managers ensure that the glue is in place and will spend time on both 'soft' and 'hard' glue. The people side to projects was considered in more detail in Chapter 8 and the 'hard' or procedural aspects are covered in Chapters 2, 3 and 7. If the project comes across barriers or problems then the formal arrangements such as contracts and regular meetings may become vital to sorting out the situation and moving the project forward.

Summary

This chapter is concerned with working in partnership. The benefits and challenges of working in partnership are explored and illustrated with examples and two detailed case studies. Project managers need to spend time creating and maintaining effective partnerships by developing the 'glue' that holds the project together. This involves active engagement in 'soft' or people-centred approaches and also ensuring that there are enabling 'hard' practices such as project contracts, explicit working practices and documentation.

References

Allen, N. and Bishoff, L. (2002) Collaborative Digitization: libraries and museums working together, *Advances in Librarianship*, **26**, 43–81.
Daker, H. (2003) The BL Reaches Out, *Library & Information Update*, **2** (10), 46–7.

Daugaard, V. (2003) The Co-operation across Cultures in Public and Scientific Libraries: the co-operation in Net Librarian. In *Access Point Library: media – information – culture, World Library and Information Congress: 69th IFLA General Conference and Council, 1–9 August 2003*, Berlin, www.ifla.org.

Horn, J. K. and Leung, S. W. (1999) *Bringing LOGIC to Local Government Information: a multi-type partnership to organize local government information*, paper presented at the Racing Towards Tomorrow Conference, organized by the Association of College and Research Libraries, 8–11 April 1999, Detroit MI, www.ala.org/Content/NavigationMenu/ACRL/.

Moody, D. (2000) *Ice Hockey, Basketball and Libraries*, www.literacytrust.org.uk/Pubs/moody.html.

National Preservation Office (2001) *Managing the Digitisation of Library, Archive and Museum Materials*, London, British Library, www.informatik.unierlangen.de/IMMD8/Lectures/DIGLIB/managing_digitization.pdf.

Pilling, S. and Kenna, S. (eds) (2002) *Co-operation in Action: collaborative initiatives in the world of information*, London, Facet Publishing.

Sullivan, H. and Skelcher, C. (2002) *Working across boundaries*, Basingstoke, Palgrave Macmillan.

10

Working on projects

Introduction

Project work provides library and information workers with an opportunity to develop their skills and experience by contributing to new and innovative activities. Projects often involve working at the 'cutting edge' of professional practice, working with technological developments and innovations, and also experiencing new and different ways of working. In many respects the project work of the last decade has become the standard practice in current library and information work, which means that getting involved in projects also provides project workers with the opportunity to be involved in creating the future. This can be extremely exciting as well as challenging.

The purpose of this chapter is to explore working on projects. Project workers may be employed solely on project work, often on a contract basis, or they may be working on a project in addition to their 'full-time' library or information role. In both of these situations individuals are faced with a range of issues that they need to tackle if they are to be effective in their role(s). This chapter looks at both types of worker. Finally the chapter considers the effective project worker and this is explored using the following themes: managing yourself, learning from experience, time management, gaining personal and career support, and using projects for career development.

The rise of the contract project worker

In line with the rise in the allocation of government and other funds through competitive tendering for projects, there has been a rise in the number of library and information staff working on fixed-term contracts. These project workers represent library and information professionals at different stages in their careers: some project workers will be at the start of their careers and use temporary relatively short-term project contracts as a means to progressing into more permanent employment; many self-employed information workers use project work as a means of building their portfolio of work and also developing their knowledge and skills; in contrast 'retired' or 'semi-retired' library and information workers may become involved in project work as a means of supplementing their income and also keeping in touch with professional activities. It is difficult to obtain accurate figures of the numbers of library and information staff currently involved in contract project work and an indication was given by a study in the higher education sector by the CHEMS Consulting and the Higher Education Consultancy Group (2002, p.3) who wrote: 'Since the Follett Report in 1993 there have been over 500 funded projects in the library and information services and these have involved at least 1,000 staff who have worked on fixed-term contracts. Most of them have had no job security beyond the project's life.' Their report gives a useful profile of ILS project staff working in the higher education sector as follows:

- 45% were aged 30–39 and 20% between 25–29.
- Most have a masters degree and very few have a PhD.
- 56% earn less than £20,000.
- 85% are full time.
- 80% are in a superannuation scheme.
- Most have been in their project for less than two years.
- 10% have permanent posts and the rest are on contract.
- 68% are on fixed-term contracts of either one year or two years in length.
- 62% of staff have worked on contracts for less than 5 years, and 26% have been engaged in similar work for 5–10 years.
- 49% of those who had worked on another project had done so in the same institution.
- 52% had never applied for a job outside higher education.
- 20% have had gaps between projects with no pay.

(CHEMS, 2002, p.20)

Why do library and information workers choose to work on projects? There are many different reasons why people choose to work on projects and informal discussions with a number of different project workers provide the following:

- 'Interest in and commitment to the subject/theme of the project.'
- 'Project looked interesting and challenging.'
- 'To develop and update skills.'
- 'To build up my portfolio of work [self-employed information worker].'
- 'To gain experience in a different sector.'
- 'Limited job opportunities within travelling distance from home.'
- 'Enjoy focusing on one area at a time.'
- 'Enjoy working at cutting edge and on innovative projects.'
- 'Enjoy flexibility of hours (no evening duty!) and opportunities to travel.'
- 'Offers a route back into professional work after a career break.'
- 'Offers an opportunity to study for a higher degree without having to pay the fees myself.'
- 'Provided an opportunity to network and re-vitalise my curriculum vitae.'
- 'To supplement pension.'

The CHEMS study found that information workers do find project work a satisfying and challenging way of working. For example one respondent in their study stated: 'I have ten years' experience in fixed term contract work, which has suited me very well. Lack of rising income is occasionally noticed, but high income has never been a motivating factor. I am able to do intelligent, innovative work among intelligent people – and that's a great thing. If contract work became as "safe", bureaucratised and controlled as much permanent work is now, it would lose much of its interest and excitement' (CHEMS, 2002, p.62).

Issues

However there are a range of issues associated with contract project work and the CHEMS Group identified the following:

- recruitment of staff
- reward
- job security
- staff development
- integration with the ILS workforce
- project closure.

Their research suggests that information workers consider project work to be an attractive career option and, as a result, there are often plenty of applicants for posts. However, recruitment is sometimes difficult for projects looking for archivists, specialist cataloguers or linguists and this sometimes causes projects to be delayed. One of the effects of the competitive bidding climate is that it pushes down salaries and the survey found that many project staff consider themselves poorly paid. The lack of a career structure within project work inhibits salary progression and project workers may work on a number of different projects without an increase in their salary. In addition, some project workers expressed concern over their conditions of service as they felt that they were not treated the same as information workers on permanent contracts.

Issues also arise as a result of the contract culture which may lead to feelings of insecurity. Many project workers are on fixed-term contracts and the study found 'strong evidence that it causes uncertainty, personal distress and leads to avoidable mobility of staff towards the end of fixed term contracts. 65% of project directors reported that staff had left early during their project. When this happens, directors suffer because of the disruption caused to the project's final months and the aggravation caused by having to find very short term replacements' (CHEMS, 2002, p.5). The following example from the CHEMS report (p.23) demonstrates a typical project career and illustrates the 'stop–start' nature of employment as a project worker:

Example   Miss X: a typical project career?

Sept 96 to Oct 99	Contract on NFF project, two extensions.
Nov 99 to Mar 00	New contract, Phase I, private donor project, one extension.
Break	Made redundant. Two months.
May 00 to Oct 00	Taken back. Contract for Donor. Phase II.
Nov 00	Three weeks' casual pay.
Nov 00 to May 01	Contract for Donor. Phase III.
May 01 to Nov 01	Contract for Special Collections RSLP Internal.
Dec 01	Post made permanent.

The CHEMS Group also identified staff development as an area for concern as although project workers regularly receive induction and technical training they are less likely to take up other forms of staff development. 'Some think they are second class citizens in terms of the benefits and support they receive from the institution. However, there is a striking ignorance about the human resource services that are available to them and only 35% of staff have been given annual appraisals or performance reviews (CHEMS, 2002, p.5). They identified that project workers were commonly involved in the following types of staff development during their employment on the project:

- technical training related to the project (64%)
- induction (54%)
- presentation skills (19%).

Other types of development were less commonly made available to contract workers. This was in part a result of the tight time frames that drive many projects as well as organizational policies that sometimes require staff to be in post for a certain period of time before they have access to some forms of staff development and also that in some ILS staff are only eligible for training and education opportunities if these are directly linked to their current role. One of the consequences of this situation is that project workers need to identify their training and development needs and work to ensure that they are met during the project process. In particular, project workers who want to move into management may be well advised to take advantage of in-house management development programmes or external programmes offered by a wide range of education and training providers, for example university-based business schools. In many universities both permanent and contract staff are able to take advantage of different educational programmes and either negotiate a fee reduction or remission.

Issues also arise with the integration of project workers and the rest of the workforce. Biddy Fisher is quoted as saying 'There is a tendency to put all the effort into getting projects funded, not into the subsequent integration of the new research staff into the workforce' (Anon, 2003, p.12). The same report quotes the experiences of one project worker as follows:

> Astrid Wissenberg spoke 'about her experiences of working in short-term projects, including one where she only met her "line-manager" eight months into the project and had no appraisal. She had also been physically located a significant distance from the library for which she was working, making contact with other staff difficult.' (Anon, 2003, p.12)

As the project comes to a close the project worker needs to start looking for new employment. The CHEMS Group (2002, p.25) asked project workers the question: 'When the project ends, what will you do?' They obtained the following responses that indicate a range of different attitudes:

- 'I will do whatever it takes to keep on working.'
- 'I will look for ways to extend the project.'
- 'I will keep on applying while on projects – no loyalty offered, no loyalty given.'
- 'I will fall into despair and disillusionment with the profession as a whole.'

Assistance with exit planning appears to be patchy and is often dependent on the goodwill and interest of individual project managers rather than organizational policies. In terms of helping themselves individual project workers can update their curriculum vitae and start looking for a new position, sign up at professional recruitment agencies run by professional associations such as CILIP and ASLIB/IMI, investigate opportunities for careers counselling, and also request a meeting with a member of staff from the human resources department and ask about the possibility of joining a redeployment register.

In addition, project workers who are on fixed-term contracts often find that their position is a lonely one as their manager's sights may be firmly fixed on achieving the project outcomes rather than helping with their staff's welfare and careers, and they may feel that they are 'on the edge' of their organization. In this type of situation mentoring can often provide a valuable source of support and career development. This is explored in a later chapter in this book.

Project workers with a full-time ILS role

In addition to project workers who are on short- or long-term contracts many ILS staff become involved in project work as part of their full-time job role. These staff may have volunteered to become involved in a project or they may have been asked to become involved as a result of working within their ILS. For example the ILS may be moving to a new building and all staff are required to become involved in planning and carrying out the move. The ILS may have successfully applied for project funding and is now implementing the project with support from its 'mainstream' staff. These examples imply that when mainstream ILS workers become involved in project work there will be a diverse range of reasons and motivations, which could include one or more of the following:

- Project clearly links with main job role.
- Worker has an interest in the project.
- The opportunity to develop and update skills.
- The worker was asked to become involved by manager.
- To gain experience in a particular area or different sector.
- The opportunity to enhance curriculum vitae and, hopefully, become more employable.
- To prevent professional stagnation.
- To network with like-minded people.
- To get out of day-to-day routine of ILS.

A common problem for project workers with a mainstream library and information role is that they become torn between the conflicting demands of their line manager and their project manager. This situation arises if there is a lack of clarity or disagreement between their work in their 'full-time' post and their project work. This can be an extremely stressful situation. The best way of ensuring that it doesn't occur is for the project worker to start off their work on the project by clarifying the needs of the project and agreeing boundaries. Sometimes a three-way meeting between project worker, project manager and ILS manager can lead to an agreement and set of boundaries for the project work.

One issue that sometimes arises with project work is that at the end of a project individuals who have been working towards a specific goal and deadlines suddenly don't have the project as part of their everyday working life. As a result they may feel quite 'flat' about their work; this can result in them becoming de-motivated, losing interest in their 'mainstream' job, and also seeking another 'more exciting' role. Sometimes the recognition that this process is taking place can reassure project workers so that they adapt to everyday working life. Some project managers are extremely aware of this process and ensure that the project workers are provided with a period of time when they 'let go' of their project work and re-engage with their everyday role. In some instances the team member has developed the 'project bug' and become committed to developing their career in project work.

Example   End of the summer

A colleague reported the impact of the end of a project in which her library and information service moved into a new building over a three-month period in the summer. All the staff involved in the project worked extremely hard to ensure that the new building and the library services were up and running in time for the return of the students early in September. During the last few weeks in August many staff voluntarily worked late and appeared to manage huge volumes of work. On 4 September the new building was ready to be open to students and staff. The staff were incredibly proud of their achievements, the ways in which they had overcome problems and also that they had achieved the project deadlines. The only outstanding work related to minor building works. However, over the next two months staff sickness and absence rates were 10% higher than normal, which the senior managers of the service saw as a response to the 'high' of the summer and the culmination of the opening of the new service. By November the situation had settled down and sickness and absence rates were back to their normal low levels.

The effective project worker

Individuals who are effective project workers are often very clear about who they are and what they want to get out of their work as well as other aspects of their lives. They are likely to pay attention to the following areas of their lives:

- managing yourself
- learning from experience
- time management
- gaining personal and career support
- using projects for career development.

Managing yourself

Managing yourself is particularly important if you are involved in project work as this is likely to introduce you to new challenges, for example new ways of working in a team, new working practices and/or technical innovations. As a result it is important to be able to manage yourself in the workplace so that you can take part in the project in a relatively stress-free way. Managing yourself involves identifying personal goals and objectives, being assertive and looking after yourself.

Identifying personal goals and objectives is about knowing where you are now and where you want to be in one, two or three years' time. Different people will be working towards their own individual goals over different timescales that suit their personal circumstances. Spending time thinking about and then writing down your personal goals is a useful way for clarifying your overall direction in life. Once you have identified your personal goal it is helpful to identify your objectives. Objectives are like stepping stones and help you to move forward to achieve your goal. Ideally objectives should be SMART (specific, measurable, achievable, realistic and time bound) and writing them down will help you to externalize them and turn them into reality. Project work offers a useful way of achieving personal objectives and also moving a career forward, revitalizing a 'tired' career or changing direction.

Once you have identified your goal then you will need to work towards it by working on the individual objectives. This may involve negotiating what you do at work, for example asking to be involved in a particular project or asking not to be involved with a piece of work. One very useful assertiveness strategy provides a six-point plan for talking about a problem with someone at work. This plan involves working through the following stages:

- Ask for time to discuss the issue.
- Identify the problem.
- Say the effect this has on you.
- Suggest a solution.
- Outline the effect of the solution.
- Thank the other person.

It is very important that you look after yourself, particularly if you are involved in demanding project work as well as working hard in your everyday job providing a service to customers.

Key aspects of looking after yourself in the workplace may include the following:

- Know your own work peaks and troughs. Most people have times of the day when they are full of energy and other times when their energy is low. For example some people are at their best in the morning (larks) while others are afternoon or evening people (owls). If you know your best times and you are able to organize when you carry out your work then it makes sense to carry out your most demanding work when your energy levels are at their highest.
- Have tea breaks and lunch breaks. Eat healthy food. When you have a break, if possible get away from your desk and get some fresh air.
- Keep your working environment clean, tidy and uncluttered.
- Use time management techniques (see summary in Figure 10.2).
- Speak to colleagues if you feel overwhelmed.
- Use breaks to network with colleagues.

Learning from experience

> Reflection is an important human activity in which people recapture your experience, think about it and mull over it and evaluate it. It is this working with experience that is important in learning. The capacity to reflect is developed at different stages in different people and it may be this ability which characterizes those who learn effectively from experience.
>
> (Boud, Keogh and Walker, 1985, p.19)

The ability to reflect on and learn from our experiences is important to everyone as it forms the basis for personal learning and change, learning and developing professional skills, and also for organizational change. It offers a way of making the most of our experiences working on projects in different contexts and it is a good way for remaining alert and responsive in a changing environment. Reflection is the basis of self-awareness and can also help identify previously unseen opportunities. An important part of the reflective process is to identify an action that you will carry out: if reflection doesn't include an action-planning process it may become mere 'navel gazing'.

Reflection in the context of project management is an important process that involves the whole project team in thinking about and learning from their experiences. Individual project workers may want to keep a project learning diary to help them to capture their project experiences and learn from them. Project learning diaries are particularly useful for capturing many of the incidents or incidental events that are soon forgotten as the project progresses. These diaries may be kept as a private and individual learning tool or as documents that will be used to inform the final project reports.

The project learning diary is meant to be a personal document: there is no right or wrong way to keep it. Find the method that suits you and remember the following points:

- Write what is important to you: it is important to be yourself.
- Be open and sincere in what you record.
- The log is a working document. As it develops, go back to earlier entries and reflect further on them, underlining, highlighting, annotating anything significant.
- Remember to date all entries.
- Don't be rigid in the way you keep your log; be prepared to change if necessary, moulding the log to your personal strengths and needs.
- Record experiences as soon as possible after they happen, but be selective; focus on experiences that are significant for you or critical to the project.

One way of ensuring that reflection takes place is to decide on a regular time at which you will write your log and a fixed time each week to reflect back on it. It is not just writing in the log that is important, but the continuing reflection on what you have written. The following questions (which are not exhaustive) may suggest things you might write about as you keep your project learning diary. Use them in ways you wish or disregard them if you prefer to. They are only intended as a stimulus to help you focus on *your* experience and *your* reflection on it.

- Are things going to plan? If not, why not? What do I need to do differently?
- How do I feel about this project, process, task or activity? What am I enjoying? What do I dislike? What do I need to do differently?
- Select a critical incident. Briefly describe it. What contributed to this situation? What was my role in creating this situation? What do I need to do differently in future?

A quick method of maintaining a project learning diary is to keep a notebook and on a daily or weekly basis write on one piece of paper which is divided into four sectors as shown in Figure 10.1. This structure is very similar to one presented in Chapter 5 on project evaluation.

Project:	Date:
What went well?	What could be improved?
What have you learnt?	What will you DO as a result of completing this diary? Be SMART

Figure 10.1 Sample structure of a project learning diary

Although the previous paragraphs relate to individual reflection using a project learning diary, the same processes may be applied to project teams. A simple way of encouraging project teams to reflect and learn from their experiences is to put this on the agenda for team meetings and allocate some time to reflection. In addition, e-mails or bulletin boards may be used to initiate and carry out reflective processes. The results of these activities can then be fed back into the project management activities and processes.

Time management

Time management appears to be an issue for many project workers and it often arises as an issue for library and information workers as a result of five main reasons:

- poor initial project planning and, particularly, the under-estimation of the time requirements of the project work
- the project manager and team being over-ambitious and taking on a project that is not appropriately resourced
- the lack of a clear agreement between the project workers and their managers about the division of time between running an ILS service and project work
- the staff being allocated too much work
- poor personal time management.

The use of the project planning techniques outlined in Chapter 3 should help prevent time management issues arising as a result of issues 1–4. One special case is that of library and information workers who are involved in working on multiple projects who sometimes find that the demands of each project peak at the same time. If this coincides with a period of high demand from the library or information service then it can lead to an extremely stressful time and the possibility that the projects and also the ILS service suffer as a result of the conflict. One important strategy to handle this situation is to manage the projects as a series of linked projects. Project management software such as MS Project provides tools that enable you to consolidate projects (see Chapter 7). Again, the issue may be avoided by detailed planning, including risk analysis.

For those people for whom personal time management is an important issue there are many books available on the topic and Figure 10.2 summarizes many of the current ideas and techniques.

1 At regular times ask yourself
- 'What is the best use of my time right now?'

2 Enquiries
- Remember to use existing materials.
- Find out how much information is required.
- Remember that 20% of your effort will achieve 80% of the results (Pareto effect).

3 Meetings
- Put time limits on agenda items.
- Put time limits on meetings.
- Attend part of a meeting, not whole meeting.
- Have meetings in rooms with no chairs.
- Hold online rather than face-to-face meetings.

4 Post
Sort your post into four groups:
- Priority. Deal with it immediately.
- Delegate to someone else.
- Hold: not important. Work through once a week/fortnight when your energy level is low.
- Useless: file in bin.

5 Self-management
- Know your own work peaks and troughs.
- Set your own calendar/schedule.
- Keep your desk clear.
- Have tea breaks and lunch breaks.
- Speak to colleagues if you feel overwhelmed.
- Use breaks to network with colleagues.

6 Workloads
- Set realistic deadlines.
- Say 'no'.
- Set targets and rewards.
- Use a daily to-do list.
- Identify what you will achieve by the end of the day.

7 E-mails and phones
- Flag up important e-mails.
- Use folder facility.
- Use voice mail.
- Axe membership of some discussion groups.

8 Interruptions
- Sign on door/closed door.
- Negotiate with the other person and book a specific time to discuss the issue.
- Minimize interruptions when completing certain tasks, e.g. report writing.
- Use a quiet room or space.
- Ask a colleague to answer your phone.

9 Paperwork
- Use Post-it ™ notes to highlight action.
- Use highlighter pens to mark out key information.

10 Prioritize
Prioritize work by organizing it under the following four headings:
- urgent and important
- important but not urgent
- urgent but not important
- not urgent and not important.
  Alternatively items in your to-do list can be assigned priority 1–4 based on these headings.

11 Team working
- Create and develop open working relationships.
- Give and receive support and feedback.
- Share difficult tasks.

12 Technology
- Spend time learning how to use relevant packages.
- Attend relevant courses or workshops.
- Be selective in the use of technology, e.g. small projects are often best managed using paper and pen rather than MS Project.

Figure 10.2 Tips and techniques for time management

Gaining personal and career support

Mentoring, which is learning by association with a role model, is an important way of gaining support in the following areas:

- moving from one project to another
- dealing with a specific issue or problem
- developing skills for a particular task or project
- training
- developing professional contacts and networks
- career and professional development.

Essentially a mentor is a friend and someone who will support our personal and career development. Some organizations have formal mentoring schemes which are typically aimed at new recruits and/or groups of staff who traditionally find barriers to their progression, for example women or staff from ethnic minorities. Informal mentoring schemes are very common and may be initiated by the mentee, their line manager or a colleague. Typically staff will identify a mentor within their own organization but some workers, e.g. consultants, find it appropriate to approach a colleague in another organization.

As a project worker it is well worthwhile considering and possibly setting up a supportive mentoring process for yourself. Think about who may be able to act as your mentor and what you want to gain from the mentoring relationship. An information worker involved in two distinct projects may work with two mentors. Typically mentoring involves meeting up with your mentor, for example at three-monthly intervals, and exploring your current situation and career plan. If you are seeking someone to mentor you as you progress from one project to another then it is important to choose someone with experience of project work and who remains up to date with new ideas and professional developments.

Working as a project manager either as a solo worker or leading a multi-skilled multi-professional team can be a demanding and challenging role. In this situation it is useful to have a mentor to whom you can go for help and support outside of the project. This may be someone within the profession who has had extensive experience of project work and may be working at a senior level within your own or another organization. The availability of someone who will give you time and space to explore your current issues and problems in confidence can be a vital source of support.

Further information about mentoring is available from a variety of sources including:

- www.libs.uga.edu/mentor/information.html
- www.mentoring.org/training/TMT/
- www.empathy-project.org.uk/.

Using projects for career development

Finally, projects are often a useful way of developing your knowledge and skills, gaining new professional experiences and also developing your network and contacts. They provide a channel through which you can develop your career and start to move towards your career goals. Project work can be used as a springboard to developing a career within ILS and also changing direction, for example many librarians are now involved in managing local government learning initiatives such as Learning Shops. Individuals who successfully use project work as a stepping stone are likely to identify the knowledge, skills and experience that they gained from their project work and use this to enhance their job application or curriculum vitae. This is illustrated in the following example.

Example   Using project work for career development

Jane worked in an academic library and was involved in a web-based project to enhance information skills in the undergraduate curriculum. She said, 'I got involved in working on the WEBPROJ as I thought it was a good way to develop my ICT skills and also make a mark in the Information Services Department. After a year's work I was really pleased with the end result and it is now used for delivering information skills to all first year students. While I was working on the WEBPROJ I became interested in e-learning and took part in an online e-learning programme offered by the university. It was a good course and opened my eyes to the possibilities of e-learning. A vacancy appeared in the university for an E-learning Officer. I wasn't going to apply for it as I didn't think I had sufficient technical expertise but my manager encouraged me. Perhaps she wanted to get rid of me! Anyway I applied and got the job. I'm enjoying my new role. It's hard work and there is a lot to learn. I have now started a Master's degree in E-learning and the university is paying for me to do it. They don't give me time off but I'm managing to fit it in and around everything else. One thing I forgot to say was that I got a good pay rise too.'

Summary

This chapter explores the experiences of project workers, differentiating between contract workers and those who work on projects alongside their mainstream ILS role. The latter will often have to deal with the challenges of working with two managers and the end of the project when they must integrate themselves back into the day-to-day work of library and information service and will perhaps miss the excitement of being involved in a project. The employment of contract workers is a permanent feature of the ILS landscape and it offers a wide range of career possibilities, often involving innovative ways of working with scope for the use of personal creativity and flexibility. A number of issues arise with contract work and these include recruitment of staff, reward, job security, staff development, integration with the ILS workforce, and project closure. Finally, this chapter considers the effective project worker from the perspectives of the following topics: managing yourself, learning from experience, time management, gaining personal and career support, and using projects for career development. The chapter ends on the note that project work may be used as a vehicle for personal career development.

References

Anon (2003) Project Workers: worry over job security, *Library & Information Update*, **2** (6), 12.

Boud, D.J., Keogh, R. and Walker, D. (eds) (1985) *Reflection: turning experience into learning*, London, Kogan Page.

CHEMS Consulting and the Higher Education Consultancy Group (2002) *Resolving the Human Issues in LIS Projects: a report to the JISC and the RSLP*, www.rslp.ac.uk/circs/.

11
Project management skills and training

Introduction

Over a decade ago projects were carried out occasionally, often as the result of a change within a local library system or in response to national initiatives. Nowadays they are part of the day-to-day working lives of many information workers and they provide an important force for library and information development and innovation. As shown earlier in this book project work offers an important route to funding both core and developmental activities in libraries and information services. These projects often involve working in new ways within multi-professional teams across traditional boundaries. Many project workers and managers are working on multiple projects.

Given the current importance of project work it is vital that library and information professionals develop the appropriate set of knowledge and skills to enable them to take part in and successfully lead and manage project work. This chapter focuses on the knowledge and skills required by project managers, and also training and education provision in this area.

Knowledge and skills required by project managers

The development of a library and information profession with appropriate knowledge and skills in project management is essential for the future of libraries and information services (both terrestrial and virtual ones) and also the profession. Simon Tanner (2003, p.34), speaking in the context of digital projects, says:

> Managers have to develop skills in the more flexible, competitive regions of project management, systems implementation and fundraising. Whatever the size of the library, there will be technology to implement, and the ability to manage the process has become a key requirement for librarians. The growth in competition for funding means that meting obligations on time and in budget is critical, not just for the task in hand but for future funding prospects as well.

Tanner identifies the skills and experience required in all next generation managers' toolkits as:

- clear vision
- stakeholder studies
- feasibility studies
- infrastructure survey
- matrix of requirements
- risk assessment.

He highlights the importance of employing the right person as the project manager and also empowering the project staff to fulfil their roles and responsibilities. He clearly states that an important risk factor in any project is losing staff, particularly at a critical stage, and this means looking after them and also providing them with plenty of staff development opportunities. Training is an important aspect of any project and Tanner quotes Paul Conway from Yale University's Project Open Book who reported the important impact of training and practice on digitization costs: 'Extensive analysis showed that the "practice effects" improved productivity 44% for scanning and 50% for indexing' (Conway as quoted by Tanner, 2003, p.36).

This view is supported by Biddy Fisher (2002) who identifies project management as an area in which library and information workers need to develop their skills. She links this with the rise in government funding to public services that 'often results in initiatives and short-term (three years is typical) projects to kick-start developments by intense activity and focus'. Her research with employers identified that they consider the following skills and/or experience as essential for library and information workers in the current environment:

- working within projects or initiatives
- creativity/imagination
- understanding the organization and the role within organization
- impact analysis
- risk taking
- lateral thinking
- scenario planning
- evidence-based practice and policy responses.

She goes on to say that 'project management skills appear to be lacking in our profession' and identifies a particular gap in skills in making bids and securing funding for projects. She mentions that project management courses, for example as provided through professional associations such as CILIP or ASLIB/IMI or via bodies such as RSLP (the Research Support Libraries Programme), do help to provide information workers with the relevant skills set.

Discussions with participants at the start of one-day project management workshops has resulted in the author identifying their perceptions of the knowledge, skills and attitudes required by project managers and these are summarized in Table 11.1. It is interesting to note that when this list is compared with that of employers (as described by Biddy Fisher above) one can see there are some topics that were not identified by the participants on the project management programmes, i.e. creativity/imagination, impact analysis, risk taking, lateral thinking, and scenario planning. One explanation could be that the workshop participants are driven by the need to develop their skills in the 'nuts and bolts' of project management and so they are not yet seeing a broader perspective on projects and their management within library and information services.

Table 11.1   Knowledge, skills and attitudes required by project managers

Knowledge	Skills
Personal	**Personal**
Own strengths and weaknesses	Assertiveness
Sources of help and support	Management of stress
	Management of uncertainty
	Time management
	Presentation skills
	Rapid reading skills
General management	**General management**
Own organization, including roles and responsibilities	Management and motivation of individuals and/or team
Politics, power and culture of organizational context(s)	Management of difficult situations and/or challenging individuals/teams
Management of people and finance	Management of change
Management of change	Ability to communicate with and influence senior managers
Legal aspects of human resource management	General communication skills
Legal issues, e.g. health and safety, copyright	Marketing and promotion
	Human resource management
Strategic management	Financial management
Project management	**Project management**
Overview of project management process	Project management tools and techniques
Sources of funding	Bids and proposal writing
Sources of information and support on general project management issues	Business plan creation
	Budget management
	Research skills, e.g. design of an evaluation process
	Risk analysis
Professional ILS	**Professional ILS**
Professional context, i.e. own ILS, ILS in other sectors	Technical expertise (ILS), e.g. archives, retrospective cataloguing, collection management
Professional networks	digitization, preservation
	Subject expertise
	Information and knowledge management
Other	**Information and communication technology skills**
Working with different professions, organizations, sectors – their context, working practices	Use of project management software
	Design and development of website
Attitudes	
Flexible; Diplomatic; Positive; Persistent; Reliable; Hardworking; Keeps promises; Enthusiastic; Creative; Unflappable; Good attention to detail	

Earlier chapters in this book have emphasized the importance of working in multi-professional teams, often across traditional boundaries. As a result library and information workers need to be able to work effectively in both traditional teams, such as those found within a particular library, and also in more complex teams, such as those found in projects that span a number of traditional sectors and professions, for example SureStart projects. This means that library and information workers need an appreciation of different types of organizations and also the cultures and values of other professional groups. They also need to understand the types of processes that are involved in enabling these teams to work effectively and efficiently together (see Chapters 8 and 9).

Biddy Fisher (2002) emphasizes the importance of information professionals being able to work in multi-skilled and collaborative teams. She highlights the importance of 'the multi-skilled team, containing members with a variety of levels of responsibility' and states that it is 'now standard practice, and flatter structures mean that individual members of staff are likely to work in several teams, depending on the focus of activity. These members of staff become multi-skilled individuals and work in new ways, often across broader departmental or organisational structures' (Fisher, 2002, p.2).

Training and education provision

Currently library and information professionals develop their professional knowledge, skills and practice through a variety of routes including:

- undergraduate or postgraduate library, information or knowledge management qualifications
- other professional qualifications, e.g. management qualifications such as the MBA
- continuing professional development activities, e.g. short courses, workshops, conferences and other professional activities
- on-the-job training and experience.

There is clearly a need for project management to be firmly located within these different professional development routes. At undergraduate and postgraduate levels students are likely to learn basic project management skills by completing individual or group assessment activities which provide them with the basic skills required for working within project teams. Other parts of their programmes will provide them with generic management and technical skills. Unfortunately the Quality Assurance Agency for Higher Education (QAA, 2000) does not explicitly mention project management in their list of knowledge and skills required by library and information workers in their benchmark statement (although they do mention the need for students to develop their skills in managing research projects). However some programmes, for example the BA (Hons) in Library and information Studies at Brighton University, do include specialist modules on project management. The majority of academic programmes include an extended project, e.g. through independent study or work placement modules, and these often enable students to gain practical experience of project management.

Professional organizations and groups often arrange short courses and events that focus on different aspect of project management including:

- generic project management skills and techniques
- project management software such as MS Project
- management of change
- implementing ICT systems
- budgeting and finance
- bidding for funds
- managing teams and individuals
- project management within a specific context, e.g. higher education
- project management of specific types of projects, e.g. digitization, e-learning.

These events are very useful in providing participants with an overview of the subject, a chance to explore and perhaps practise different skills and techniques, and the opportunity to look at case studies and effective practice in other library and information units. One of the main benefits of attending is that they provide the participant with an opportunity to share ideas and experiences with other practitioners, and to make contacts with people with relevant experiences. These types of events are organized by the professional associations such as CILIP and ASLIB/IMI, and also by specialist professional groups such as RSLP. Library and information workers in the voluntary sector will also have an opportunity to attend events organized by learning and development teams in local, regional or national voluntary and community groups. These events are often available at a very low fee or free of charge to people working in the voluntary or community sector.

Conferences also provide an important opportunity for professional updating, and for individuals at the start of their career it is a useful way of gaining an overview of a topical theme or issue. For people who are active players in a field it can be a way of gaining valuable nuggets of information and exchanging ideas with others. Meeting with other project managers or team members is an important means of networking, sharing common problems (and solutions) and gaining a new perspective on one's own project and its progress. In the author's experience the process of participating in a conference, whether it is attending presentations or workshops or chatting to people in the inevitable coffee queue, often sparks off new ideas and connections which lead to new approaches to tackling old problems on one's return to the workplace. The exhibitions that stand alongside the main conference activities often provide access to up-to-date information on a variety of information systems and they are also a useful source of free pens, mugs and other novelties!

Finally, many project managers learn their project management skills and experience on the job. A key factor to ensure that this is a successful learning process is to spend time planning, talking with and learning from colleagues (both within ILS and in the profession as a whole). Reading this book and others like it (see list of resources in Appendix B) will provide a good starting point, as will joining in relevant professional activities, networks and discussion groups. As discussed in Chapter 10, many project managers find it extremely useful to work with a mentor who will be able to provide advice, guidance and support both in terms of the current project and also future career possibilities. The active use of a Career Development Portfolio enables individual managers to capture their learning and to then use this in future projects (and also job applications). A Career Development Portfolio is a simple file (paper-based or electronic) which someone uses to record their career and it is likely to contain their curriculum vitae, examples of work, e.g. presentations, reports or papers, results of questionnaires such as learning styles or skills assessment, certificates, and an individual learning journal. Individuals may structure their portfolio in their own way or use the help and support of their professional organization such as CILIP.

Summary

The field of project management has developed from its foundation in the world of scientific management to one which brings together the 'art' of managing people, change and complex systems and also the 'science' of a wide range of project management tools and methodologies. Project management brings a range of challenges to library and information workers and also the opportunity for creative thinking and working. Projects are now embedded in the day-to-day working of libraries and information units. Today's projects are likely to hold within them the seeds of tomorrow's practice in librarianship and information work and, as a result, they offer individuals and teams the possibility of making a difference and influencing professional practice.

Project management is now a core activity for many library and information professionals. As a result it is important that new graduates leave library school with basic project management tools and techniques. Practising information workers need opportunities to develop their knowledge and skills in this area too. Professional associations and groups provide an extensive range of opportunities for continuous professional development in project management.

References

Fisher, B. (2002) Skills for the Future Information Professional: the role of individuals, educators, professional bodies and employees. In Fraser, M. (ed.), *The Vital Link 3: staffing in library and information services in the 21st Century: Proceedings of the Third National Staffing Conference, 29–30 November 2002*, University of South Australia.

QAA (2000) *Librarianship and Information Management*, www.qaa.ac.uk.

Tanner, S. (2003) Next Generation Managers, *Library & Information Update*, **2** (12), 34–6.

Appendix A
The language of funding

For ILS workers who have not previously ventured into the world of funding it may appear as if they have walked into a strange new world with its own language. Getting to grips with this language is important and an essential activity for any project manager who is working on or hoping to work on an externally funded project. This section provides a summary of many of the important terms, based, in part, on the work of Adirondack (1998).

The people involved in finance

Accountant

Someone who will provide financial advice and/or manage your financial records and provide appropriate financial information in an appropriate format, e.g. for auditing purposes.

Auditor

Someone who will audit or check the 'paper-trail' and ensure that the project money has been spent in an appropriate way and as outlined in the contract.

Beneficiaries

Individuals who benefit from the funding, e.g. as customers in the ILS service or individuals who attend training courses or sessions funded by the project.

Donor, funder or sponsor

An individual or organization that provides money for projects or other ventures. Donors are individuals who give or raise donations, e.g. from individuals or organizations. A funder or sponsor is normally an organization that provides grants or funds (or other forms of support).

Project manager

> The person who is responsible for managing the finances, maintaining the financial records and reporting the financial situation to their manager, management group or steering committee.

Reviewer

> An individual who is involved in checking a grant application and ensuring that it matches the criteria of the funding organization. They will then evaluate the application and make a recommendation on its acceptance or otherwise.

The funding process

Assessment or review process

> The funding application will normally be assessed by either a committee or number of individuals. Their role is to check the funding application against their criteria for funding and grade it. Funding applications that achieve the highest grade, i.e. that are the closest match to the funder's criteria, are those that are likely to be successful.

Budget

> A summary of the project finances, including the costs of everything and also any income.

Contract

> A legally binding and legally enforceable agreement between the funder and the recipient organization. Adirondack (1998, p.85) states that for

> a contract to exist in law there must be:

> - unconditional offer and acceptance by both (or all) parties to the contract, so every side both offers something and receives something
> - consideration, which means that something of material value – goods, services, money, or the promise of any of those – is given in exchange for goods or services
> - the intention to create a legally binding relationship.

> Contracts are normally written down although verbal contracts do exist.

Funding application

A request for money from a sponsor or funder. Many funders require that funding applications are written to a specific structure and format. Funding organizations will often provide an application form or pro forma, and these may be available in print-based or electronic format.

Funding programme

Many funders offer a limited range of funding programmes (or opportunities), each one focusing on a particular theme or need. The focus of the funding programmes is likely to change over time.

Funding stream

An amount of money (often millions) that has been allocated to a particular initiative or set of initiatives, e.g. digitization, e-learning. Funding streams are often established over a three- to five-year period and there will be a timetabled programme of funding programmes or projects within this stream.

Grants

The money that is available from donors, funders or sponsors to assist projects or other ventures; they may be for general purposes or a specific purpose. They vary in size from extremely small, e.g. £100, through to major with some grants amounting to millions of pounds. Grants may be provided by a statutory authority, charitable trust, professional association or other body. The funding organization will often set conditions on the recipient of the grant, e.g. on how and when the money is spent, and on the types of reports it expects to receive from the recipient, e.g. monthly financial reports, milestone reports. Sometimes grants are also called grant aid agreements or grant aid contracts.

Joint venture

This is where public and private organizations agree to work together on an equal basis, e.g. each organization putting up some funding and the profits being jointly shared.

Public–private partnership (PPP)

A relationship between a public and private sector organization. This may be an informal relationship or a contractual one.

Service agreement

A service agreement or service level agreement refers to an agreement in which one body agrees to provide a specific service. The service agreement is likely to detail the specification of the service, e.g. service requirements, performance indicators. A service agreement may be agreed between two departments in the same organization (an in-house agreement) or between different organizations. The service agreement may be written into a grant or contract.

Different types of funding

Gap funding

Sometimes the costs of the project aren't covered by a single funder and there is a gap in funding. This gap may be filled by obtaining money from another funder or donor, or it may be provided by the organization who is bidding for funding.

Match funding

Match funding takes place when the funding provided by an external agency, e.g. the European Social Fund (ESF) or Research Support Libraries Programme (RSLP), is 'matched' by funding provided by other organizations, who may be the institution bidding for funding, or another source, perhaps in the private sector. The ratio of match funding may vary, e.g. ESF projects have a ratio of 48%/52%, RSLP may contribute no more than 70% of the total amount (Milne, 2002). Funding organizations such as ESF, English Partnership and some of the lottery boards all require match funding.

Partnership funding

Sometimes the money obtained or offered by a single funder doesn't cover the total costs of a project and in this situation funds may be obtained from partners, e.g. organizations involved in the project and its outcomes. Partnership funding is often a requirement of public funding organizations.

Different methods of payment

Block payment

Here the grant is paid in blocks, e.g. at set stages in the project. Some funders will provide a block payment to start up the project and then pay regular sums of money, e.g. at monthly or three-monthly intervals. This is one of the commonest methods of payment.

Cost and volume

In this situation a payment is made for an agreed volume or amount of service and additional payments priced by volume are made if additional services are required or if the number of users exceeds an agreed level.

Unit pricing or price by case

In this instance the funder pays an agreed price per unit of provision. An example of a unit of provision could be the availability of one computer with internet access for library users.

References

Adirondack, S. (1998) Just About Managing: effective management for voluntary organisations and community groups, 3rd edn, London, LVSC.

Milne. R. (2002) Joined Up Funding: promoting and facilitating collaborative work. In Pilling, S. and Kenna, S. (eds), Co-operation in Action: collaborative initiatives in the world of information, Facet Publishing, 121–36.

LIBRARY, UNIVERSITY COLLEGE CHESTER

Appendix B
Resources

Audit Commission (1998) *A Fruitful Partnership: 'Effective Partnership Working'*, London, Audit Commission Management Paper.

Brown, M. (1998) *Successful Project Management in a Week*, 2nd edn, London, Hodder and Stoughton.

Burke, R. (2003) *Project Management. Planning and control techniques*, 4th edn, Chichester, Wiley.

CCTA (2002) *Managing Successful Projects with Prince 2*, Central Computer and Telecommunications Agency, London, HMSO.

Fisher, K. and Fisher, M. D. (2001) *The Distance Manager*, New York, McGraw-Hill.

Gallacher, C. (1999) *Managing Change in Libraries and Information Services*, London, ASLIB/IMI.

Leigh, A. and Walters, M. (1998) *Effective Change: 20 ways to make it happen*, 2nd edn, London, CIPD.

Lock, D. (1992) *Project Management*, 5th edn, Aldershot, Gower.

MacLachlan, L. (1996) *Making Project Management Work for You*, London, Library Association Publishing.

Maitland, I. (2000) *Budgeting for Non-Financial Managers*, Harlow, Pearson.

Maylor, H. (1996) *Project Management*, London, Pitman Publishing.

Pugh, L. (2000) *Change Management in Information Services*, Aldershot, Gower.

Slack, N., Chambers S. and Johnston, R. (2000) *Operations Management*, 3rd edn, London, Financial Times/Prentice Hall.

Turner, J. R. (ed.) (2003) *Contracting for Project Management*, Aldershot, Gower.

Turner, J. R. (ed.) (2003) *People in Project Management*, Aldershot, Gower.

Wren, A. (2003) *The Project Management A–Z*, Aldershot, Gower.

Young, T. L. (1998) *The Handbook of Project Management: a practical guide to effective policies and procedures*, 2nd edn, London, Kogan Page.

Index